# Python Metaprogramming:

A Comprehensive Guide to Building Efficient, Extensible, and Adaptable Applications Through Dynamic Code Generation and Other Advanced Techniques

By
**Charles J. Drake**

# Table Of Contents

# CHAPTER 1

## Unveiling the Power of Python Metaprogramming

---

*Beyond the Usual: Crafting Code That Writes Code*

If you're just starting your programming journey, this might sound a bit unusual at first, but don't worry! We'll break it down into simple, digestible pieces.

At its core, **metaprogramming is the art of writing code that manipulates other code**.

Think of it like this:

- In regular programming, you write code, and that code works with *data*. For example, you might write code to take a list of numbers and sort them, or code to take a sentence and count the words.
- In metaprogramming, your code also works with *code* itself. This means you can write code that reads, changes, or even creates other code.

It's like being a programmer and a code-architect at the same time. You're not just building a house; you're also designing the tools and blueprints that are used to build houses.

To make this clearer, let's explore the key aspects:

## 1. What Exactly Is Metaprogramming?

To put it formally, metaprogramming is a programming technique where programs can treat other programs (or even themselves) as their data. This allows you to write code that can:

- **Inspect Code:** Look at the structure of other code.
- **Analyze Code:** Understand what the code does.
- **Transform Code:** Change the code to do something else.
- **Generate Code:** Create new code from scratch.

## 2. Key Concepts in Metaprogramming

There are a few fundamental ideas that underpin metaprogramming. Let's explore them:

- **Introspection:**
    - This is the ability of a program to examine its own structure and properties during runtime.
    - In simpler terms, it's like a program being able to "look in the mirror" and understand what it's made of.
    - This includes things like:
        - Knowing the types of objects it's working with (e.g., is this a number, a string, or a list?).
        - Discovering the attributes and methods of those objects (e.g., what data does this object hold, and what actions can it perform?).

- Even examining its own source code.
  - Python is very strong in introspection. It provides several built-in functions and modules to make this easy. We'll explore this in detail in **Chapter 2: Diving Deep into Python's Introspection Capabilities**.
- **Dynamic Code Generation:**
  - This is the process of creating new code while the program is running.
  - Instead of writing all your code beforehand, you can write code that generates code as needed.
  - This might sound strange, but it's incredibly powerful. Imagine being able to create functions or classes on the fly, based on user input or changing conditions.
  - Python provides tools like the exec() statement and the eval() function to help with this. We'll cover these in **Chapter 3: Dynamic Code Execution with exec() and eval()**.
- **Code Modification:**
  - Metaprogramming isn't just about creating new code; it's also about changing existing code.
  - This allows you to adapt and extend the behavior of your code without directly editing the original source code.
  - For example, you could add extra functionality to a function or a class without changing its core definition.
  - Python offers several ways to modify code, including:

- **Decorators:** These are a way to "wrap" functions or classes with extra behavior. We'll explore them in **Chapter 4: Mastering Code Modification with Decorators**.
- **Metaclasses:** These are advanced tools that allow you to control how classes themselves are created. This opens up a lot of possibilities for customizing class behavior, as we'll see in **Chapter 5: The Magic of Metaclasses: Controlling Class Creation**.

### 3. Paradigms Within Metaprogramming

While metaprogramming is a broad concept, there are some common approaches and patterns:

- **Reflection:**
  - This is closely related to introspection. It's the ability of a program to examine and modify its own structure and behavior.
  - In Python, reflection is a natural part of how the language works. Objects, classes, and functions are all first-class citizens, meaning they can be inspected and manipulated at runtime.
- **Generative Programming:**
  - This focuses on the creation of code based on some kind of template or specification.
  - Instead of writing code directly, you write a "generator" that produces the code for you.

- o Dynamic code generation is a key part of this.
- **Aspect-Oriented Programming (AOP):**
  - o This is a programming paradigm that aims to increase modularity by allowing the separation of *cross-cutting concerns*.
  - o Cross-cutting concerns are functionalities that apply to many different parts of a program, such as logging, security, or transaction management.
  - o While Python doesn't have built-in AOP in the same way some other languages do, metaprogramming techniques, especially decorators, can be used to achieve similar results.

Metaprogramming might seem like a complex topic, but hopefully, you now have a better grasp of the fundamental concepts. It's all about writing code that can manipulate other code, enabling you to create more flexible, powerful, and adaptable programs. As you progress through this book, you'll see how these ideas translate into practical techniques and real-world applications.

*Supercharging Your Python: The Efficiency, Extensibility, and Adaptability Advantage*

Let's explore in more detail why you might want to use metaprogramming in Python. While it might add some complexity, the benefits it brings to **efficiency, extensibility, and adaptability** are substantial, especially for larger and more complex projects.

## 1. Efficiency: Doing More with Less Code

- **The Problem of Repetition:** In many programming scenarios, you'll find yourself writing similar code over and over again. This could be creating variations of a class, defining similar functions with slight differences, or handling repetitive tasks like logging or data validation. This repetition leads to:
    - **Increased Codebase Size:** More code means more files, more lines to read, and a larger surface area for potential bugs.
    - **Maintenance Overhead:** When you need to change something, you have to find and modify every instance of the repeated code, increasing the risk of errors and making updates time-consuming.
    - **Reduced Readability:** Repetitive code makes it harder to see the essential logic of your program, as it's buried under a mountain of duplication.
- **How Metaprogramming Helps:** Metaprogramming provides tools to automate this repetitive code generation. Instead of writing the same code multiple times, you write code that *generates* that code for you.
- **Benefits of Metaprogramming for Efficiency:**
    - **Reduced Codebase:**
        - Metaprogramming allows you to achieve more with fewer lines of code. For example, you can write a function or a class that dynamically generates other functions or classes, rather than writing each one out individually.

- A smaller codebase is easier to manage, understand, and debug. It reduces the cognitive load on developers, making it simpler to grasp the overall structure and logic of the application.
  - **Faster Development:**
    - By automating code generation, you eliminate the manual effort involved in writing repetitive code. This speeds up the development process, allowing you to focus on the unique and essential aspects of your application.
    - Tools like decorators and metaclasses can automate common tasks, such as adding logging, validation, or error handling to multiple functions or classes with minimal code.
  - **Potential for Optimized Performance:**
    - In some cases, metaprogramming can lead to performance improvements. For instance, you can generate specialized code that is tailored to a specific use case, rather than relying on generic code that handles multiple scenarios.
    - This specialized code can be more efficient because it avoids unnecessary checks or operations.

## 2. Extensibility: Building Systems That Grow Gracefully

- **The Challenge of Change:** Software applications are rarely static. They need to evolve over time to accommodate new features, changing requirements, and expanding user bases. Designing applications that can be easily extended is crucial for long-term success.
- **The Limitations of Traditional Approaches:** In traditional programming, extending an application often involves modifying existing code, which can be risky and disruptive. It can introduce bugs, break compatibility with existing components, and make future updates more difficult.
- **How Metaprogramming Helps:** Metaprogramming provides powerful mechanisms for creating systems that are designed to be extended without requiring modifications to the core codebase.
- **Benefits of Metaprogramming for Extensibility:**
  - **Plugin Architectures:**
    - Metaprogramming enables the creation of plugin-based systems, where new functionality can be added by plugging in external modules or components.
    - Dynamic module loading (a key metaprogramming technique) allows the application to discover and load new code at runtime, without requiring the application to be restarted or recompiled. We'll cover this in **Chapter 8: Building Extensible Applications with Metaprogramming**.
  - **Automated Registries:**

- Metaclasses can be used to automatically register new classes or components with a central registry. This makes it easy to discover and use available extensions.
- For example, you could define a metaclass that automatically registers any new class that inherits from a particular base class, making them available to other parts of the application. This reduces the need for manual configuration and ensures that new extensions are automatically recognized by the system.

- **Configuration-Driven Behavior:**
  - Metaprogramming allows you to create applications whose behavior can be customized through external configuration files or data, rather than through code changes.
  - This means you can modify the application's functionality without having to modify and redeploy the code, making it more flexible and adaptable to different environments and user needs. We'll see this in **Chapter 8: Building Extensible Applications with Metaprogramming**.

## 3. Adaptability: Responding to Changing Needs

- **The Dynamic Nature of Software:** Software often operates in dynamic environments where conditions can change frequently. These changes might include variations in data formats, different user preferences, or the need to integrate with diverse external systems.

- **The Difficulty of Static Code:** Code that is written statically at development time can be inflexible and difficult to adapt to these changing conditions.
- **How Metaprogramming Helps:** Metaprogramming enables code to adapt its structure and behavior at runtime, allowing it to respond dynamically to changing circumstances.
- **Benefits of Metaprogramming for Adaptability:**
  - **Dynamic Class Creation:**
    - You can create classes on the fly, tailoring their attributes and methods to specific data or runtime conditions.
    - For example, if your application needs to work with different data sources, each with its own structure, you can use metaprogramming to create classes that are specifically designed to handle each data source.
  - **Runtime Code Modification:**
    - Techniques like decorators make it possible to modify the behavior of existing functions or classes without altering their original source code.
    - This allows you to add or change functionality dynamically, depending on the situation.
  - **Framework and Library Development:**

- Many popular Python frameworks and libraries leverage metaprogramming to provide a high degree of flexibility and adaptability to their users.
- For example, a web framework might use metaprogramming to dynamically route requests to different handlers based on URL patterns, or an ORM (Object-Relational Mapper) might use it to map database tables to Python classes.

*Core Principles of Dynamic Code Generation and Introspection*

Let's delve deeper into the two fundamental pillars of Python metaprogramming: dynamic code generation and introspection.

## 1. Dynamic Code Generation: Building Code on the Fly

- **The Essence of Code Creation**: Dynamic code generation is the process of constructing new code during the execution of a program. Instead of writing code that is fixed at the time of development, you write code that can create other code as the program runs. This generated code can then be executed to perform specific tasks.
- **How it Works**:
    - At its most basic, dynamic code generation involves creating strings that contain Python code.

- These strings can represent anything from simple expressions to complex functions, classes, or even entire modules.
- Once the code string is constructed, it can be executed using built-in Python functions like exec() or eval().

- **Key Concepts and Techniques**:
  - exec(object[, globals[, locals]]): This function executes a block of Python code, which can be a string, a code object, or a file object. It's a powerful tool for executing multi-line code or code with side effects (e.g., defining functions or classes). We'll cover this in detail in Chapter 3: Dynamic Code Execution with exec() and eval().
    - Example:

```
code_string = "def greet(name): print(f'Hello, {name}!')"
exec(code_string) # Define the function
greet("Alice")      # Call the function
```

  - eval(expression[, globals[, locals]]): This function evaluates a single Python expression. It's useful for dynamically calculating values or determining the result of a computation. See more in Chapter 3: Dynamic Code Execution with exec() and eval().
    - Example:

```
expression = "2 + 3 * 4"
result = eval(expression)
print(result) # Output: 14
```

- **String Formatting**: String formatting techniques (e.g., f-strings, .format()) are crucial for constructing code strings with dynamic content.
  - Example:

```
variable_name = "user_age"
value = 30
code_string = f"{variable_name} = {value}"
exec(code_string)
print(user_age)  # Output: 30
```

- **Abstract Syntax Trees (ASTs)**: For more advanced code generation, you can use the ast module to represent code as a tree-like structure. This allows you to analyze and modify code in a more structured and reliable way than by manipulating strings directly. We'll explore this in Chapter 7: Transforming Code with Abstract Syntax Trees (AST).
- **Use Cases and Benefits**:
  - Generating boilerplate code: You can write code that automatically generates repetitive code patterns, reducing redundancy and improving maintainability.
  - Creating dynamic functions or classes: You can define functions or classes with behavior that is determined at runtime, based on data or external conditions.
  - Building domain-specific languages (DSLs): You can create specialized languages tailored to a particular problem domain, making your code

more expressive and easier to understand for specific tasks.

- ○ Configuration-driven applications: Generate code or modify behavior based on configuration files.

## 2. Introspection: Examining the Inner Workings of Code

- **The Ability to Look Within**: Introspection is the capability of a program to examine its own structure and properties during runtime. It allows your code to "look inside" itself and discover information about its objects, functions, classes, and modules.
- **How it Works**: Python provides a rich set of built-in functions and modules that enable introspection. These tools allow you to query the attributes, methods, types, and other characteristics of program elements.
- **Key Concepts and Techniques**:
  - ○ type(object): Returns the type of an object. This is fundamental for understanding what kind of data you're working with.
    - ■ Example:

```
x = 10
print(type(x))  # Output: <class 'int'>
```

    - ■
  - ○ dir(object): Returns a list of the names of the attributes and methods of an object. This helps you discover what an object can do.
    - ■ Example:

```
my_list = [1, 2, 3]
print(dir(my_list))
# Output: ['__add__', '__class__', ..., 'append', 'clear', ...]
```

■

- getattr(object, name[, default]): Gets the value of a named attribute of an object.
  - Example:

```
class MyClass:
    my_attribute = "Hello"

obj = MyClass()
value = getattr(obj, "my_attribute")
print(value)  # Output: Hello
```

■

- setattr(object, name, value): Sets the value of a named attribute of an object.
- hasattr(object, name): Checks if an object has a given named attribute.
- isinstance(object, classinfo): Checks if an object is an instance of a given class or a tuple of classes.
- issubclass(class, classinfo): Checks if a class is considered a subclass of another class.
- inspect module: This module provides a wide range of functions for getting information about live objects, including modules, classes, functions, methods, and stack frames. It's a powerful tool for deep introspection. We dive into this in Chapter 2: Diving Deep into Python's Introspection Capabilities.
  - Example:

```python
import inspect

def my_function(a, b):
    """This is a docstring."""
    pass

print(inspect.signature(my_function))
# Output: (a, b)
print(inspect.getdoc(my_function))
# Output: This is a docstring.
```

- **Use Cases and Benefits**:
  - Debugging and error handling: Introspection can help you understand the state of your program and identify the cause of errors.
  - Dynamic dispatch: You can use introspection to determine which method to call on an object at runtime, based on its type or attributes.
  - Object serialization and deserialization: Introspection can be used to examine the attributes of an object and convert them to a format suitable for storage or transmission.
  - Plugin systems: Introspection can help you discover and load plugins dynamically.
  - Automated documentation generation: You can use introspection to extract documentation strings from your code and generate API documentation.
  - Testing: Introspection can be used to examine the properties of objects and verify that they meet certain conditions.

## A First Look at Python's Metaprogramming Tools and Techniques

Python provides a rich set of tools and techniques that allow you to engage in metaprogramming. Here, we'll introduce the primary ones, setting the stage for a more in-depth exploration in the later sections of this book.

### 1. Introspection Tools

- As discussed in the previous section on "Core Principles of Dynamic Code Generation and Introspection," introspection is the ability of a program to examine its own structure and properties at runtime. Python offers several built-in functions and modules for this purpose.
- **Key Introspection Tools:**
    - type(object): This function returns the type of an object. It's a fundamental tool for understanding the nature of the data you're working with.
        - Example:

```
x = 42
print(type(x))  # Output: <class 'int'>


y = "Hello"
print(type(y))  # Output: <class 'str'>
```

    ■

    - dir(object): This function returns a list of names (attributes and methods) belonging to an object. It's helpful for discovering what an object can do.
        - Example:

```
my_list = [1, 2, 3]
print(dir(my_list))
```

```
# Output:
# [..., 'append', 'clear', 'copy', 'count', 'extend', 'index',
# 'insert', 'pop', 'remove', 'reverse', 'sort', ...]
```

■

- o getattr(object, name[, default]): This function gets the value of a named attribute of an object. If the attribute doesn't exist, it can return a default value (if provided) or raise an AttributeError.
  - ■ Example:

```
class MyClass:
    my_attribute = "Python"


obj = MyClass()
value = getattr(obj, "my_attribute")
print(value)  # Output: Python

value_missing = getattr(obj, "missing_attribute", None)
print(value_missing)  # Output: None
```

■

- o setattr(object, name, value): This function sets the value of a named attribute of an object. If the attribute doesn't exist, it will be created.
  - ■ Example:

```
class MyClass:
    pass


obj = MyClass()
setattr(obj, "new_attribute", 100)
print(obj.new_attribute)  # Output: 100
```

■

- hasattr(object, name): This function checks if an object has a given named attribute. It returns True if the attribute exists, and False otherwise.
  - Example:

```
class MyClass:
    my_attribute = "Example"


obj = MyClass()
has_attr = hasattr(obj, "my_attribute")
print(has_attr)  # Output: True

has_attr_missing = hasattr(obj, "missing_attribute")
print(has_attr_missing)  # Output: False
```

- isinstance(object, classinfo): This function checks if an object is an instance of a given class (or a tuple of classes).
  - Example:

```
my_list = [1, 2, 3]
print(isinstance(my_list, list))  # Output: True
print(isinstance(my_list, tuple))  # Output: False
```

- issubclass(class, classinfo): This function checks if a class is considered a subclass of another class (or a tuple of classes).
  - Example:

```
class ParentClass:
    pass


class ChildClass(ParentClass):
```

```
    pass

print(issubclass(ChildClass, ParentClass))  # Output: True
print(issubclass(ParentClass, ChildClass))  # Output: False
```

■

- ○ inspect module: This module provides a comprehensive set of functions for gathering information about various Python objects, including modules, classes, functions, methods, and more. It's particularly useful for more advanced introspection tasks. We dedicate **Chapter 2: Diving Deep into Python's Introspection Capabilities** to this module.
  - ■ Example:

```
import inspect

def sample_function(arg1, arg2="default"):
    """This is a docstring for sample_function."""
    pass

# Get the signature of the function
signature = inspect.signature(sample_function)
print(signature)  # Output: (arg1, arg2='default')

# Get the docstring of the function
docstring = inspect.getdoc(sample_function)
print(docstring)    # Output: This is a docstring for
sample_function.
```

■

- We'll explore these tools in greater detail in **Chapter 2: Diving Deep into Python's Introspection Capabilities**.

## 2. Dynamic Code Execution

- Python allows you to execute code that is generated or provided at runtime. This capability is provided by the exec() and eval() functions.
- **Key Dynamic Code Execution Tools:**
  - exec(object[, globals[, locals]]): This function executes a block of Python code. The code can be in the form of a string, a code object, or a file object.
    - Example:

```python
code_string = """
def multiply(x, y):
  return x * y


result = multiply(5, 10)
print(result)
"""
exec(code_string)  # Executes the code and prints 50
```

  ■

  - eval(expression[, globals[, locals]]): This function evaluates a single Python expression.
    - Example:

```python
expression = "10 + 5"
result = eval(expression)
print(result)  # Output: 15
```

  ■

- A thorough discussion of these functions, including their uses and potential security concerns, is provided in **Chapter 3: Dynamic Code Execution with exec() and eval()**.

### 3. Decorators

- Decorators provide a way to modify or extend the behavior of functions or methods without changing their actual code. They use the @ symbol followed by the decorator name and are applied to the function or method definition.
- **Key Points:**
  - Decorators are essentially syntactic sugar for wrapping a function or method with another function.
  - They can be used to add functionality such as logging, memoization, authentication, and more.
  - Decorators can also be applied to classes to modify their behavior.
- Example:

```
def my_decorator(func):
    def wrapper(*args, **kwargs):
        print("Before calling the function")
        result = func(*args, **kwargs)
        print("After calling the function")
        return result
    return wrapper


@my_decorator
def say_hello(name):
```

```
   print(f"Hello, {name}!")
   return "Greeting complete"

say_hello("Alice")
# Output:
# Before calling the function
# Hello, Alice!
# After calling the function
```

- Decorators are covered in detail in **Chapter 4: Mastering Code Modification with Decorators**.

## 4. Metaclasses

- Metaclasses are a more advanced metaprogramming tool that allows you to control the creation of classes themselves.
- **Key Points:**
    - A metaclass defines how a class behaves. Just as a class is a blueprint for creating objects, a metaclass is a blueprint for creating classes.
    - By default, Python uses the built-in type metaclass.
    - You can create custom metaclasses to customize the class creation process, enforce coding standards, or add functionality to classes automatically.
- Example:

```
class MyMeta(type):
   def __new__(cls, name, bases, attrs):
      print(f"Creating class: {name}")
```

```
    # Modify attributes here, e.g., add a new method
    attrs['extra_attribute'] = "Added by metaclass"
    return super().__new__(cls, name, bases, attrs)

class MyClass(metaclass=MyMeta):
  class_attribute = "Original"

  def my_method(self):
    print("Method from MyClass")

obj = MyClass()
print(obj.extra_attribute)  # Output: Added by metaclass
```

- Metaclasses are discussed in detail in **Chapter 5: The Magic of Metaclasses: Controlling Class Creation**.

## 5. Attribute Access Control

- Python provides special methods that allow you to intercept and customize how attributes are accessed, set, or deleted.
- **Key Methods:**
    - __getattr__(self, name): Called when an attribute is accessed but not found in the object's instance dictionary.
    - __setattr__(self, name, value): Called when an attribute is set.
    - __delattr__(self, name): Called when an attribute is deleted.
- **Descriptors**: The descriptor protocol (__get__, __set__, __delete__) provides a powerful way to manage

attribute access, often used for creating properties, implementing data validation, and more.

- These techniques are covered in **Chapter 6: Fine-Grained Control with Attribute Access and Descriptors**.

## 6. Abstract Syntax Trees (ASTs)

- Abstract Syntax Trees (ASTs) represent the structure of your code in a tree-like format. The ast module in Python allows you to interact with ASTs.
- **Key Points:**
    - You can use the ast module to analyze Python code programmatically.
    - You can traverse and modify the AST to change the structure of the code.
    - This is useful for tasks like code analysis, code transformation, and generating code.
- Example:

```python
import ast

# Parse a code string into an AST
code_string = "x = 10 + 5"
tree = ast.parse(code_string)

# Print the AST (for demonstration)
print(ast.dump(tree))

# You can now traverse and modify the tree
# (Example: change 10 to 20)
```

```
for node in ast.walk(tree):
    if isinstance(node, ast.Num) and node.n == 10:
        node.n = 20

# Generate code from the modified AST
import astor  # You might need to install this: pip install astor
modified_code = astor.to_source(tree)
print(modified_code)  # Output: x = 20 + 5
```

- We explore ASTs in **Chapter 7: Transforming Code with Abstract Syntax Trees (AST)**.

This overview provides a foundation for understanding the primary tools and techniques you'll encounter in Python metaprogramming. Each of these will be explored in greater depth in its own chapter.

*Use Cases and Real-World Examples of Python Metaprogramming*

Metaprogramming might seem like an abstract concept, but it has numerous practical applications in Python development. Let's explore some key use cases and real-world examples, focusing on how metaprogramming contributes to efficiency, extensibility, and adaptability.

### 1. Efficient Code Generation

- **Reducing Boilerplate Code:**
    - Many programming tasks involve writing repetitive code with slight variations.

Metaprogramming can automate the generation of this boilerplate, saving significant development time and reducing the risk of errors.

- **Example: Data Serialization**
  - When working with different data formats (like JSON, XML, or database records), you often need to write code to serialize (convert data to a specific format) and deserialize (convert data from a format back to objects) objects.
  - Metaprogramming can be used to generate this serialization/deserialization code automatically based on the structure of your classes.
  - Instead of writing separate serialization functions for each class, you define a generic mechanism that uses introspection to examine class attributes and generate the necessary code.
  - This approach is more efficient because you write less code, and it's more maintainable because changes to your class structure are automatically reflected in the serialization code.

- **Optimizing Performance:**
  - In some cases, metaprogramming can be used to generate highly specialized code that is optimized for a particular task.
  - **Example: Creating Optimized Functions**

- Imagine you have a system that performs complex calculations with many parameters. Using metaprogramming, you can analyze the specific values of those parameters at runtime and generate a function that is tailored to those values.
- This generated function can be more efficient than a generic function that needs to handle all possible parameter combinations.

## 2. Building Extensible Systems

- **Plugin Architectures:**
  - Metaprogramming is crucial for creating applications that support plugins, allowing you to add new functionality without modifying the core application.
  - **Example: Dynamic Module Loading**
    - A common approach is to use dynamic module loading, where the application discovers and loads external modules at runtime.
    - You can use introspection to examine the modules and find classes or functions that implement a specific interface.
    - This allows you to create a flexible system where users can extend the application's functionality by simply adding new modules.

- **Automated Registration:**
  - Metaclasses can automate the process of registering components or classes with a central registry, making it easier to extend and configure applications.
  - **Example: Class Registration**
    - Suppose you're building a system with various types of data processors. You can define a metaclass that automatically registers each new processor class with a central registry.
    - This registry can then be used to look up and instantiate the appropriate processor based on user input or configuration.
    - This eliminates the need for manual registration and reduces the chances of errors.

## 3. Adaptable Applications

- **Dynamic Configuration:**
  - Metaprogramming enables applications to adapt their behavior based on external configuration or data, without requiring code changes.
  - **Example: Dynamic Class Creation from Configuration**
    - Consider an application that interacts with various external APIs, each with a different data structure.

- Instead of defining separate classes for each API response, you can use metaprogramming to create classes dynamically based on the API's response schema.
- This allows your application to adapt to changes in the API without requiring code modifications.

- **Code Generation for Different Environments:**
  - Software often needs to run in different environments (e.g., development, testing, production), each with its own specific settings or requirements.
  - Metaprogramming can generate code tailored to each environment.
  - **Example: Database Connection Handling**
    - You might have different database connection settings for each environment. Using metaprogramming, you can generate code that uses the appropriate connection parameters based on the current environment.

## 4. Frameworks and Libraries

- Many popular Python frameworks and libraries leverage metaprogramming to provide a high degree of flexibility and ease of use.
  - **Example: Django ORM (Object-Relational Mapper)**

- Django's ORM uses metaclasses to define the mapping between Python classes and database tables. When you define a Django model, the ORM uses metaprogramming to create database tables, generate query methods, and perform other database-related operations.
- This allows developers to interact with databases using Python code, without writing raw SQL queries.
    - **Example: Flask Web Framework**
        - Flask uses decorators extensively for defining routes, handling requests, and other web-related tasks.
        - Decorators simplify the process of creating web applications and make the code more readable and concise.

By automating code generation, enabling dynamic behavior, and providing tools for introspection and modification, metaprogramming empowers developers to create Python applications that are more efficient, extensible, and adaptable to changing requirements.

# CHAPTER 2

# *Diving Deep into Python's Introspection Capabilities*

---

*Understanding Python Objects at Runtime: Types, Attributes, and Methods*

In Python, everything is an object. This fundamental principle means that data and code are treated uniformly, allowing for powerful and flexible programming techniques. To truly grasp metaprogramming and dynamic behavior, it's essential to understand how Python objects work at runtime.

### 1. Objects: The Building Blocks

- **Definition:** An object is a fundamental unit of data and code in Python. It's an entity that has:
    - **Identity:** A unique identifier that distinguishes it from other objects (obtained via the id() function).
    - **Type:** Determines the kind of object it is and the operations it supports (obtained via the type() function).
    - **Value:** The data that the object represents.
- **Analogy:** Think of an object as a box.
    - The box has a unique serial number (identity).
    - The box is of a specific type (e.g., a box for books, a box for clothes).

o The box contains specific items (value).

## 2. Types: Classifying Objects

- **What are Types?** A type, also known as a class, determines the structure and behavior of an object. It defines:
    - o The kind of data the object can hold (attributes).
    - o The operations that can be performed on the object (methods).
- **Built-in Types:** Python provides a rich set of built-in types, including:
    - o Numeric types: int, float, complex
    - o Sequence types: list, tuple, str, range
    - o Mapping type: dict
    - o Set types: set, frozenset
    - o Boolean type: bool
    - o And many more.
- **Classes and User-Defined Types:** You can define your own types using the class keyword. These user-defined types are also classes.
    - o Example:

```python
class Dog:
  def __init__(self, name, breed):
    self.name = name
    self.breed = breed

  def bark(self):
    print("Woof!")
```

```
my_dog = Dog("Buddy", "Golden Retriever")
print(type(my_dog))  # Output: <class '__main__.Dog'>
```
   - ○

- The type() Function: The type() function is crucial for introspection. When called with an object, it returns the object's type.
  - ○ Example:

```
x = 10
print(type(x))  # Output: <class 'int'>

y = "Hello"
print(type(y))  # Output: <class 'str'>

def my_function():
  pass
print(type(my_function)) # Output: <class 'function'>
```
  - ○

- **Types are also objects:** In Python, types themselves are objects. Specifically, they are instances of a metaclass (by default, the type metaclass). This is a key concept in metaprogramming, as it allows you to manipulate class creation. We'll dive into metaclasses in Chapter 5: The Magic of Metaclasses: Controlling Class Creation.

## 3. Attributes: Data Associated with Objects

- **What are Attributes?** Attributes are data associated with an object. They represent the object's state or characteristics.
  - ○ **Instance attributes:** Specific to a particular instance of a class.

- o **Class attributes:** Shared by all instances of a class.
- **Accessing Attributes:** You access attributes using dot notation (object.attribute_name).
  - o Example:

```
class Circle:
    pi = 3.14159  # Class attribute

    def __init__(self, radius):
        self.radius = radius  # Instance attribute

my_circle = Circle(5)
print(my_circle.radius) # Access instance attribute
print(Circle.pi)        # Access class attribute
```
  - o

- **Dynamic Attributes:** Python allows you to add, modify, or delete attributes at runtime. This dynamic nature contributes to Python's flexibility.
  - o Example:

```
class Person:
    pass

person = Person()
person.name = "Alice" # Add attribute dynamically
person.age = 30
print(person.name, person.age) # Output: Alice 30

del person.age      # Delete attribute
# print(person.age) # Raises AttributeError
```
  - o

- The getattr(), setattr(), and hasattr() Functions: These built-in functions provide more flexible ways to work with attributes, especially when you don't know the attribute name beforehand. We touched on these in the previous section "A First Look at Python's Metaprogramming Tools and Techniques", and we'll see them again in Chapter 2: Diving Deep into Python's Introspection Capabilities.
  - getattr(object, name[, default]): Gets the value of an attribute.
  - setattr(object, name, value): Sets the value of an attribute.
  - hasattr(object, name): Checks if an object has a specific attribute.

## 4. Methods: Functions Associated with Objects

- **What are Methods?** Methods are functions that are associated with an object. They define the operations that an object can perform.
  - **Instance methods:** Operate on a specific instance of a class (and have self as the first parameter).
  - **Class methods:** Bound to the class, not the instance (and have cls as the first parameter, and are defined with the @classmethod decorator).
  - **Static methods:** связаны с классом, но не требуют ссылки на экземпляр или класс (определяются с помощью декоратора @staticmethod).

- **Calling Methods:** You call methods using dot notation (object.method_name()).
    - Example:

```
class Car:
    def __init__(self, make, model):
        self.make = make
        self.model = model

    def start(self):  # Instance method
        print(f"The {self.make} {self.model} is starting.")

    @classmethod
    def get_number_of_wheels(cls): # Class method
        return 4

    @staticmethod
    def get_car_type(): # Static method
        return "Vehicle"

my_car = Car("Toyota", "Camry")
my_car.start()  # Call instance method
print(Car.get_number_of_wheels()) # Call class method
print(Car.get_car_type()) # Call static method
```

## 5. How This Relates to Metaprogramming

- Understanding how objects, types, attributes, and methods work at runtime is crucial for metaprogramming because it allows you to:
    - **Inspect objects:** Use introspection to examine an object's type, attributes, and methods. This is

essential for tasks like serialization, dynamic dispatch, and generating code based on object structure.

- ○ **Modify object behavior:** Dynamically add, modify, or delete attributes and methods. This enables you to adapt objects to changing conditions or extend their functionality.
- ○ **Control class creation:** Metaclasses allow you to control how classes are created, giving you the power to enforce patterns, automatically add functionality to classes, or create classes dynamically.

By manipulating these fundamental aspects of Python objects at runtime, metaprogramming makes it possible to write code that is more flexible, adaptable, and efficient.

*Exploring the type() Function and its Role in Metaclasses*

The type() function in Python is more than just a way to check an object's type. It's also the key to understanding how classes are created and how metaclasses work. Let's delve into this dual role.

1. The Dual Role of type()

- **Getting an Object's Type:**
  - ○ When you call type() with a single argument (an object), it returns the type of that object.
  - ○ Example:

```
x = 10
print(type(x))  # Output: <class 'int'>

y = "Hello"
print(type(y))  # Output: <class 'str'>
```

- **Creating a New Class:**
    - The type() function can also be used to create a new class dynamically.
    - It takes three arguments:
        - name: The name of the new class.
        - bases: A tuple of base classes from which the new class inherits.
        - dct: A dictionary containing the attributes and methods of the new class.

    - Example:
```
MyClass = type('MyClass', (object,), {
    'x': 10,
    'my_method': lambda self: self.x * 2
})

obj = MyClass()
print(obj.x)        # Output: 10
print(obj.my_method()) # Output: 20
```

    - In this example, type() is used to create a class named MyClass with an attribute x and a method my_method.

## 2. Understanding Metaclasses

- **Classes are Objects:** In Python, classes are first-class objects, just like instances of classes. This means you can pass classes as arguments to functions, assign them to variables, and create them dynamically.
- **Metaclasses are the "Classes of Classes":**
    - Just as instances are created from classes, classes are created from metaclasses.
    - A metaclass defines how a class should behave. It's the blueprint for creating classes.
    - By default, the type class is Python's default metaclass. So, when you define a class using the class keyword, Python uses type to create that class.
- **The Class Creation Process:**
    - When you define a class using the class keyword, Python does the following:
        1. Executes the class body (the code within the class block).
        2. Collects the class attributes and methods into a dictionary.
        3. Calls the metaclass (by default, type) with the class name, base classes, and the dictionary of attributes.
        4. The metaclass's __new__ method creates the class object.
        5. The metaclass's __init__ method initializes the class object.

## 3. Role of type() in Metaclasses

- type as the Default Metaclass: The type class is the default metaclass in Python. This means that by default, all classes are instances of type.
- **Customizing Class Creation:** To customize the class creation process, you create a custom metaclass by inheriting from type and overriding its __new__ or __init__ methods.
- How type() is involved: When a class is created, the type() function's __new__ method (or the overridden __new__ method in a custom metaclass) is responsible for creating the class object in memory.
- Example:

```python
class MyMeta(type):
    def __new__(cls, name, bases, dct):
        print(f"Creating class {name}")
        # Modify the class dictionary here
        modified_dct = {
            key.upper(): value for key, value in dct.items()
        }
        return super().__new__(cls, name, bases, modified_dct)

class MyClass(metaclass=MyMeta):
    x = 10
    y = 20

obj = MyClass()
```

```
print(MyClass.X)    # Output: 10 (attribute name is now
uppercase)
```

- In this example, MyMeta is a custom metaclass. When
  MyClass is created, MyMeta's __new__ method is
  called, which modifies the class attributes to be
  uppercase.

**4. Metaclasses and Dynamic Class Creation**

- Metaclasses enable you to create classes dynamically,
  controlling their behavior and structure at runtime.
- This is useful for:
    - **Generating classes based on data:** You can
      create classes with attributes and methods
      determined by data from a database, API, or
      configuration file.
    - **Enforcing coding standards:** You can use
      metaclasses to ensure that all classes in a project
      adhere to certain naming conventions or have
      specific attributes or methods.
    - **Implementing design patterns:** Metaclasses can
      help automate the implementation of design
      patterns like Singleton or Abstract Base Class.
    - **Creating domain-specific languages (DSLs):**
      Metaclasses can be used to define the structure
      and behavior of classes in a DSL.

The type() function is fundamental to both inspecting object
types and creating classes. Metaclasses, which are classes that
create classes, leverage type() to customize the class creation

process. This powerful combination enables dynamic class creation, allowing for highly flexible and adaptable code.

## Using dir(), vars(), getattr(), setattr(), and hasattr() for Object Inspection

Python provides several built-in functions that allow you to inspect the properties and behavior of objects at runtime. These functions are essential for metaprogramming and for building systems that can adapt to changing conditions. Let's explore them in detail:

1. dir(object=None)

- **Purpose:** The dir() function returns a list of names in the current scope or a list of valid attributes of an object.
- **How it Works:**
  - If called without arguments, it returns the names in the current local scope.
  - If called with an object as an argument, it attempts to return a list of that object's valid attributes.
- **What it Reveals:** The list may contain names of:
  - Attributes (variables)
  - Methods (functions)
  - Classes
  - Modules
- **Example:**

```
class MyClass:
    class_attribute = 10
```

```python
    def __init__(self, instance_attribute):
        self.instance_attribute = instance_attribute

    def my_method(self):
        pass

obj = MyClass(20)

print(dir(obj))
# Output (roughly):
# ['__class__', '__delattr__', '__dict__', '__dir__', '__doc__',
#       '__eq__',    '__format__',    '__ge__',    '__getattr__',
'__getattribute__',
# '__gt__', '__hash__', '__init__', '__init_subclass__', '__le__',
# '__lt__', '__ne__', '__new__', '__reduce__', '__reduce_ex__',
#       '__repr__',    '__setattr__',    '__sizeof__',    '__str__',
'__subclasshook__',
#       '__weakref__',    'class_attribute',    'instance_attribute',
'my_method']

print(dir(MyClass))
# Output (roughly): same as above, but without
'instance_attribute'
```

- **Relevance to Adaptability and Extensibility:** dir() is useful for discovering the capabilities of an object at runtime. This allows your code to dynamically determine what attributes and methods are available, making it adaptable to different object types or changing object structures.

2. vars(object=None)

- **Purpose:** The vars() function returns the __dict__ attribute of a module, class, instance, or any other object with a __dict__ attribute.
- **How it Works:**
  - If called with a module, class, or instance, it returns a dictionary containing the object's attributes.
  - If called without arguments, vars() acts like locals().
- **What it Reveals:** The dictionary contains:
  - Keys: Attribute names
  - Values: Corresponding attribute values
- **Example:**

```
class MyClass:
  class_attribute = 10

  def __init__(self, instance_attribute):
    self.instance_attribute = instance_attribute

  def my_method(self):
    pass

obj = MyClass(20)
```

```
print(vars(obj))
# Output: {'instance_attribute': 20}

print(vars(MyClass))
# Output (roughly):
# {'__module__': '__main__', '__dict__': <attribute '__dict__'
of 'MyClass' objects>,
#    '__weakref__': <attribute '__weakref__' of 'MyClass'
objects>,
#    '__doc__': None, 'class_attribute': 10, 'my_method':
<function MyClass.my_method at 0x...>}
```

- **Relevance to Adaptability and Extensibility:** vars() allows you to access an object's attributes as a dictionary, which can be useful for:
  - Serializing object data
  - Dynamically modifying object state
  - Processing objects with unknown structures

3. getattr(object, name[, default])

- **Purpose:** The getattr() function returns the value of a named attribute of an object.
- **How it Works:**
  - Takes an object and an attribute name as a string.
  - If the object has the attribute, its value is returned.
  - If the object does not have the attribute:
    - If a default value is provided, it is returned.
    - Otherwise, an AttributeError is raised.
- **Example:**

```
class MyClass:
    my_attribute = "Hello"

obj = MyClass()

value1 = getattr(obj, "my_attribute")
print(value1)  # Output: Hello

value2 = getattr(obj, "missing_attribute", None)
print(value2)  # Output: None

# value3 = getattr(obj, "missing_attribute")
# Raises AttributeError
```

- **Relevance to Adaptability and Extensibility:** getattr()
  enables you to access attributes dynamically, without
  knowing their names in advance. This is crucial for:
    - Handling objects with varying sets of attributes
    - Implementing flexible data access mechanisms
    - Interacting with external systems or data sources

4. setattr(object, name, value)

- **Purpose:** The setattr() function sets the value of a
  named attribute of an object.
- **How it Works:**
    - Takes an object, an attribute name as a string, and
      a value.
    - If the object has the attribute, its value is updated.

- If the object does not have the attribute, it is created and assigned the given value.
- **Example:**

```
class MyClass:
    pass

obj = MyClass()

setattr(obj, "my_attribute", "World")
print(obj.my_attribute)  # Output: World

setattr(obj, "another_attribute", 123)
print(obj.another_attribute)  # Output: 123
```

- **Relevance to Adaptability and Extensibility:** setattr() allows you to modify an object's attributes dynamically, which is useful for:
  - Adapting object state based on runtime conditions
  - Implementing dynamic configuration
  - Building systems that can be extended with new attributes

5. hasattr(object, name)

- **Purpose:** The hasattr() function checks if an object has a given named attribute.
- **How it Works:**
  - Takes an object and an attribute name as a string.

- ○ Returns True if the object has the attribute, False otherwise.
- **Example:**

```
class MyClass:
    my_attribute = "Example"

obj = MyClass()

has_attr1 = hasattr(obj, "my_attribute")
print(has_attr1)  # Output: True

has_attr2 = hasattr(obj, "missing_attribute")
print(has_attr2)  # Output: False
```

- **Relevance to Adaptability and Extensibility:** hasattr() allows you to check for the existence of an attribute before attempting to access it, preventing AttributeError exceptions and enabling you to write more robust and adaptable code.

## *HERE ARE MORE EXAMPLES & CODE SNIPPETS TO SOLIDIFY YOUR UNDERSTANDING OF OBJECT INSPECTION FUNCTIONS*

Here are more detailed examples to illustrate how dir(), vars(), getattr(), setattr(), and hasattr() are used for object inspection in Python.

1. dir() Examples

- **Example 1: Inspecting a Module**

```python
import math  # Import the math module

print(dir(math))
# Output (excerpt):
# ['__doc__', '__name__', '__package__', 'acos', 'acosh', 'asin', 'asinh',
# 'atan', 'atan2', 'atanh', 'ceil', 'comb', 'copysign', 'cos', 'cosh',
# 'degrees', 'dist', 'e', 'erf', 'erfc', 'exp', 'expm1', 'fabs', 'factorial',
# 'floor', 'fmod', 'frexp', 'fsum', 'gamma', 'gcd', 'hypot', 'inf', 'isclose',
# 'isfinite', 'isinf', 'isnan', 'isqrt', 'lcm', 'ldexp', 'log', 'log10',
# 'log1p', 'log2', 'modf', 'nan', 'nextafter', 'perm', 'pi', 'pow', 'prod',
# 'radians', 'remainder', 'sin', 'sinh', 'sqrt', 'tan', 'tanh', 'tau', 'trunc']
# This example shows how dir() can be used to list the
# functions and constants available in the math module.
```

- **Example 2: Inspecting a User-Defined Class**

```python
class Dog:
    """A simple class representing a dog."""

    species = "Canis familiaris"  # Class attribute, shared by all instances

    def __init__(self, name, breed, age):
        self.name = name  # Instance attribute: name of the dog
```

```python
    self.breed = breed  # Instance attribute: breed of the dog
    self.age = age  # Instance attribute: age of the dog

def bark(self):
    """Makes the dog bark."""
    print("Woof!")

def get_description(self):
    """Returns a description of the dog."""
        return f"{self.name} is a {self.breed} and is {self.age} years old."

my_dog = Dog("Buddy", "Golden Retriever", 3)  # Create an instance of the Dog class
print(dir(Dog))
print(dir(my_dog))
# In this example, dir(Dog) shows class attributes and methods,
# while dir(my_dog) shows instance-specific attributes in addition to the class attributes.
```

2. vars() Examples

- **Example 1: Instance Attributes**

```python
class Person:
    def __init__(self, name, age, city):
        self.name = name  # Instance attribute: name of the person
```

```python
    self.age = age  # Instance attribute: age of the person
    self.city = city  # Instance attribute: city of the person

person1 = Person("Alice", 30, "New York")   # Create an
instance of the Person class
print(vars(person1))  # Output: {'name': 'Alice', 'age': 30, 'city':
'New York'}
# Here, vars() provides a dictionary of the instance's attributes.
```

- **Example 2: Module Attributes**

```python
import math  # Import the math module

print(vars(math))
# This will show the attributes of the math module as a
dictionary.
```

3. getattr() Examples

- **Example 1: Accessing an Attribute Safely**

```python
class Book:
    def __init__(self, title, author, pages):
        self.title = title  # Instance attribute: title of the book
        self.author = author  # Instance attribute: author of the
book
        self.pages = pages  # Instance attribute: number of pages
in the book
```

```python
book1 = Book("Python Crash Course", "Eric Matthes", 544)  #
Create an instance of the Book class

# Accessing an existing attribute
title = getattr(book1, "title")   # Get the value of the 'title'
attribute
print(title)  # Output: Python Crash Course

# Accessing a non-existing attribute with a default value
publisher = getattr(book1, "publisher", "Unknown Publisher")
# Get 'publisher', or 'Unknown Publisher' if it doesn't exist
print(publisher)  # Output: Unknown Publisher

# Accessing a non-existing attribute without a default value
# publisher_error = getattr(book1, "publisher")
# Raises AttributeError: 'Book' object has no attribute
'publisher'
# This demonstrates how to use the optional default argument
to avoid errors.
```

- Example 2: Using getattr() in a loop

```python
class Configuration:
    def __init__(self, **kwargs):
        for key, value in kwargs.items():
            setattr(self, key, value)  # Dynamically set attributes
based on keyword arguments

config_data = {
    "host": "localhost",
```

```
    "port": 8080,
    "timeout": 10,
}
config    =    Configuration(**config_data)      #   Create   a
Configuration object with data

for attr_name in ["host", "port", "timeout"]:
    attr_value = getattr(config, attr_name)  # Dynamically get
the value of each attribute
    print(f"{attr_name}: {attr_value}")
```

4. setattr() Examples

- **Example 1: Setting and Updating Attributes**

```
class Circle:
    def __init__(self, radius):
        self.radius = radius  # Instance attribute: radius of the
circle

circle1 = Circle(5)  # Create an instance of the Circle class

# Set a new attribute
setattr(circle1, "color", "red")   # Set the 'color' attribute to
"red"
print(circle1.color) # Output: red

# Update an existing attribute
```

```python
setattr(circle1, "radius", 10)  # Update the 'radius' attribute to
10
print(circle1.radius)  # Output: 10
```

- **Example 2: Dynamic Attribute Assignment**

```python
def create_object(class_name, attributes):
    """Dynamically creates an object with given attributes."""
    obj = type(class_name, (object,), {})()  # Create an empty
object of the specified class
    for key, value in attributes.items():
        setattr(obj, key, value)  # Set attributes dynamically for
the new object
    return obj


my_object = create_object("DynamicObject", {"name":
"John", "age": 25, "city": "London"})
print(my_object.name)  # Output: John
print(my_object.age)  # Output: 25
print(my_object.city)  # Output: London
```

5. hasattr() Examples

- **Example 1: Checking for Attribute Existence**

```python
class Product:
    def __init__(self, name, price):
        self.name = name  # Instance attribute: name of the
product
        self.price = price  # Instance attribute: price of the product
```

```python
product1 = Product("Laptop", 1200)  # Create an instance of
the Product class

if hasattr(product1, "price"):  # Check if the 'price' attribute
exists
    print("Price attribute exists.")  # Output: Price attribute
exists.
else:
    print("Price attribute does not exist.")

if hasattr(product1, "quantity"):  # Check if the 'quantity'
attribute exists
    print("Quantity attribute exists.")
else:
    print("Quantity attribute does not exist.")  # Output:
Quantity attribute does not exist.
```

- Example 2: Using hasattr() for conditional logic

```python
class Message:
    def __init__(self, text, sender=None):
        self.text = text  # Instance attribute: text of the message
        self.sender = sender  # Instance attribute: sender of the
message (optional)

def print_message_details(message):
    print(f"Text: {message.text}")
    if hasattr(message, "sender"):  # Check if the 'sender'
attribute exists
```

```
    print(f"Sender: {message.sender}")
  else:
    print("Sender: N/A")

message1 = Message("Hello")
message2 = Message("Hi", "Alice")

print_message_details(message1)
print_message_details(message2)
```

## Practical Applications in Building Adaptable and Extensible Systems

- **Dynamic Configuration:** You can use these functions to load configuration data from external sources (e.g., files, databases) and dynamically set object attributes based on that configuration. This allows your application to adapt to different environments or user preferences without modifying the code.
- **Plugin Systems:** You can use introspection to discover and load plugins at runtime. hasattr() and getattr() can be used to check if a plugin provides the required attributes or methods, and then call those methods dynamically.
- **Data Validation:** You can use hasattr() and getattr() to check if an object has the necessary attributes before processing it, ensuring data integrity and preventing errors.
- **Object Serialization and Deserialization:** vars(), getattr(), and setattr() can be used to dynamically access

and manipulate object attributes when converting them to or from formats like JSON or XML.

- **Dynamic Dispatch:** You can use getattr() to retrieve a method of an object by its name at runtime, allowing you to choose which method to call based on runtime conditions or user input.

By using these functions effectively, you can create systems that are more flexible, robust, and capable of adapting to evolving requirements.

*The Power of inspect Module: Examining Callables, Modules, and Classes*

The inspect module in Python is a powerful tool for introspection, providing a wide range of functions to get information about live objects in a running program. It's incredibly useful for understanding the structure and behavior of your code at runtime, which is crucial for advanced techniques like metaprogramming, debugging, and building extensible applications.

**1. Core Concepts**

- **Introspection:** The ability of a program to examine its own structure and properties. The inspect module is Python's primary tool for performing introspection.
- **Live Objects:** The inspect module works with objects as they exist in memory during program execution. This allows you to see the actual state of your code, not just its static representation.

- **Callables:** Objects that can be called (e.g., functions, methods, classes).
- **Modules:** Python code organized into files.
- **Classes:** Blueprints for creating objects.

## 2. Examining Callables

The inspect module provides several functions to get information about callable objects:

- inspect.isfunction(object): Checks if an object is a Python function.
- inspect.ismethod(object): Checks if an object is a bound method (a method associated with an instance of a class).
- inspect.isbuiltin(object): Checks if an object is a built-in function or method (e.g., len(), str.upper()).
- inspect.isroutine(object): Checks if an object is a user-defined or built-in function or method.
- inspect.getsource(object): Returns the source code of a function or method.
- inspect.signature(object): Returns a Signature object representing the call signature of a callable, including parameters and return type.
- inspect.getdoc(object): Retrieves the docstring of a callable.

  o **Example:**

```python
import inspect
```

```python
def greet(name: str, greeting: str = "Hello") -> str:
    """Greets a person with an optional greeting."""
    return f"{greeting}, {name}!"

class MyClass:
    def instance_method(self, x: int) -> int:
        return x * 2

    @classmethod
    def class_method(cls, y: int) -> int:
        return cls.class_attribute + y

    @staticmethod
    def static_method(z: int) -> int:
        return z + 1

obj = MyClass()

# Examining the greet function
print(inspect.isfunction(greet))  # True
print(inspect.getsource(greet))
print(inspect.getdoc(greet))
print(inspect.signature(greet))

# Examining methods of MyClass
print(inspect.ismethod(obj.instance_method))  # True
print(inspect.ismethod(MyClass.class_method))  # False
print(inspect.isbuiltin(len)) # True
```

```
print(inspect.signature(MyClass.instance_method))
print(inspect.signature(MyClass.class_method))
print(inspect.signature(MyClass.static_method))
```

## 3. Examining Modules

The inspect module also provides functions to get information about modules:

- inspect.ismodule(object): Checks if an object is a module.
- inspect.getmembers(object[, predicate]): Returns all the members of an object (e.g., functions, classes, variables) as a list of (name, value) pairs. The optional predicate argument can be used to filter the members (e.g., inspect.isclass).
- inspect.getmodulename(path): Returns the module name for a given file path.
    - **Example:**

```
import inspect
import math

print(inspect.ismodule(math))  # True

math_members = inspect.getmembers(math)
print(len(math_members))  # Number of members in the math module

# Get all classes defined in the math module
```

```
math_classes = [
    name for name, value in inspect.getmembers(math) if
inspect.isclass(value)
]
print(math_classes)
```

## 4. Examining Classes

You can use the inspect module to explore the structure and inheritance of classes:

- inspect.isclass(object): Checks if an object is a class.
- inspect.getmro(cls): Returns a tuple of class objects in the order they are searched during method resolution (Method Resolution Order or MRO).
- inspect.getmembers(object[, predicate]): As mentioned earlier, this is very useful for getting class members.
- inspect.getclasstree(classes, unique=False): Get the class hierarchy in a list of class objects.
- inspect.getfullargspec(func): useful for getting the arguments of the __init__ method.
  - **Example:**

```
import inspect

class BaseClass:
    pass

class MyClass(BaseClass):
    class_attribute = 10

    def __init__(self, x, y):
```

```
        self.x = x
        self.y = y

    def my_method(self, z):
        pass

print(inspect.isclass(MyClass))  # True

# Get the Method Resolution Order
mro = inspect.getmro(MyClass)
print(mro)

# Get all members of MyClass
members = inspect.getmembers(MyClass)
print(members)

# Get the arguments of the __init__ method
init_signature = inspect.getfullargspec(MyClass.__init__)
print(init_signature)
```

## 5. Significance for Metaprogramming

The inspect module is invaluable for metaprogramming because it allows you to:

- **Dynamically analyze code:** You can examine the structure of classes, functions, and modules at runtime, enabling you to make decisions about how to proceed.
- **Modify behavior:** By understanding the attributes and methods of objects, you can use functions like setattr() to modify them dynamically.

- **Generate code:** You can use the information obtained from inspect to generate new code or adapt existing code.

## 6. Use Cases

- **Debugging:** The inspect module can help you understand the state of your program and track down errors.
- **Framework development:** Frameworks like Django and Flask use inspect to provide features like dynamic routing, automatic form processing, and more.
- **Plugin systems:** You can use inspect to discover and load plugins dynamically.
- **Documentation generation:** Tools like Sphinx use inspect to extract docstrings and generate API documentation.
- **Testing:** You can use inspect to examine the properties of objects during testing.

*HERE ARE MORE EXAMPLES & CODE SNIPPETS TO SOLIDIFY YOUR UNDERSTANDING OF USING THE INSPECT MODULE*

Here are some expanded examples to demonstrate the use of the inspect module in more detail, with a focus on the concepts discussed in the previous section.

## 1. Examining Callables

- **Example 1: Inspecting a Function's Signature**

```
import inspect
```

```python
def calculate_area(radius: float, pi: float = 3.14159) -> float:
    """Calculates the area of a circle."""
    return pi * radius**2

signature = inspect.signature(calculate_area)
print(signature)
# Output: (radius: float, pi: float = 3.14159) -> float

for param in signature.parameters.values():
    print(f"Parameter Name: {param.name}")
    print(f"Parameter Type: {param.annotation}")
    print(f"Parameter Default: {param.default}")
    print(f"Parameter Kind: {param.kind}")

return_annotation = signature.return_annotation
print(f"Return Annotation: {return_annotation}")
```

This example shows how to use inspect.signature() to get information about a function's parameters and return type.

- **Example 2: Inspecting a Method's Source Code**

```python
import inspect

class Rectangle:
    def __init__(self, width: float, height: float) -> None:
        """Initializes a rectangle with width and height."""
        self.width: float = width
        self.height: float = height

    def area(self) -> float:
```

```
        """Calculates the area of the rectangle."""
        return self.width * self.height

print(inspect.getsource(Rectangle.area))
# Output:
#     def area(self) -> float:
#         """Calculates the area of the rectangle."""
#         return self.width * self.height
```

This example retrieves the source code of the area method of the Rectangle class.

## 2. Examining Modules

- **Example 1: Getting Module Members**

```
import inspect
import random

# Get all members of the random module
random_members = inspect.getmembers(random)
print(f"Number    of    members    in    random    module:
{len(random_members)}")

# Filter for functions in the random module
random_functions = [
        name for name, value in random_members if
inspect.isfunction(value)
]
print(f"Functions in random module: {random_functions}")
```

This example demonstrates how to use inspect.getmembers()
to get a list of members in a module and filter them based on
their type.

- **Example 2: Examining a custom module**

```python
# Create a dummy module in a file called my_module.py
with open("my_module.py", "w") as f:
    f.write("""
\"\"\"This is a sample module.\"\"\"

def my_function(x):
    \"\"\"A sample function.\"\"\"
    return x + 1

my_variable = 10

class MyClass:
    \"\"\"A sample class.\"\"\"
    class_attribute = 5
    def __init__(self,instance_attribute):
        self.instance_attribute = instance_attribute

    def my_method(self, y):
        return y * 2

""")

import inspect
import my_module
```

```python
print(inspect.ismodule(my_module))

print(inspect.getdoc(my_module))
print(inspect.getsource(my_module))

print(inspect.getmembers(my_module))
```

## 3. Examining Classes

- Example 1: Exploring Class Hierarchy with inspect.getmro()

```python
import inspect
from typing import List, Type

class Animal:
    pass

class Mammal(Animal):
    pass

class Dog(Mammal):
    pass

class GoldenRetriever(Dog):
    pass

def print_mro(cls: Type) -> None:
    """Prints the Method Resolution Order of a class."""
    mro_list: List[Type] = inspect.getmro(cls)
    print(f"Method Resolution Order for {cls.__name__}:")
```

```
    for base_class in mro_list:
        print(base_class.__name__)

print_mro(GoldenRetriever)
```

This example uses inspect.getmro() to show the inheritance order for the GoldenRetriever class.

- Example 2: Getting Class Members and __init__ Arguments

```
import inspect

class Person:
    """Represents a person with name, age, and address."""

    class_attribute: str = "Person"  # Class Attribute

    def __init__(self, name: str, age: int, address: str) -> None:
        """
        Initializes a Person object.

        Args:
            name: The person's name.
            age: The person's age.
            address: The person's address.
        """
        self.name: str = name
```

```python
        self.age: int = age
        self.address: str = address

    def greet(self) -> str:
        """Returns a greeting message."""
        return f"Hello, my name is {self.name}."

# Get members of the Person class
person_members = inspect.getmembers(Person)
print("Members of Person class:")
for name, value in person_members:
    print(f"{name}: {value}")

# Get the arguments of the __init__ method
init_signature = inspect.signature(Person.__init__)
print("\n__init__ signature:")
for param in init_signature.parameters.values():
    print(f"  {param.name}: {param.annotation}")
```

## Practical Examples of Introspection for Debugging, Analysis, and Dynamic Behavior

The inspect module is not just for academic curiosity; it's a powerful tool in practical Python programming. Here's how you can use it to enhance your debugging, analysis, and code's dynamic behavior:

### 1. Debugging

- **Understanding the Call Stack**
  When an exception occurs, Python provides a traceback,

which shows the sequence of function calls that led to the error. However, you can also use inspect to examine the call stack at any point in your program, even without an exception. This can be incredibly helpful for understanding the flow of execution and identifying the origin of unexpected behavior.

- o inspect.stack(): Returns a list of frame records for the caller's stack.
- o inspect.currentframe(): Returns the frame object for the caller's frame.

```python
import inspect

def function_a():
    frame_info = inspect.currentframe()
    print(f"Current function: {frame_info.f_code.co_name}")
    print(f"Line number: {frame_info.f_lineno}")
    function_b()

def function_b():
    stack = inspect.stack()
    print("Call stack:")
    for frame_info in stack:
        print(f"    File: {frame_info.filename}, Line: {frame_info.lineno}, Function: {frame_info.function}")

function_a()
```

- In this example, inspect.stack() in function_b allows you to see the entire call stack, showing that function_a called function_b. This can be very useful for tracing the execution path in complex code.

- Inspecting Variables in a Frame
  You can use the inspect module in conjunction with the frame object to access the local variables within a function's scope.

```python
import inspect

def my_function(arg1, arg2):
    local_variable = "hello"
    frame = inspect.currentframe()
    local_vars = frame.f_locals
    print(f"Local variables: {local_vars}")
    return arg1 + arg2

my_function(5,10)
```

## 2. Analysis

- Analyzing Function Signatures
  The inspect.signature() function allows you to analyze the parameters of a function, which is useful for validating arguments, generating function calls, or creating adaptable function wrappers.

```python
import inspect

def process_data(data: list, transform: str = "default",
output_format: str = "json") -> dict:
```

```python
    """Processes data based on specified transformations and
output format."""
    # Implementation details...
    return {}

sig = inspect.signature(process_data)

for name, param in sig.parameters.items():
    print(f"Parameter: {name}")
    print(f"  Type: {param.annotation}")
    print(f"  Default: {param.default}")
    print(f"  Kind: {param.kind}")  # Positional_or_keyword,
variable_positional, etc.

print(f"Return type: {sig.return_annotation}")
```

- This example shows how to use inspect.signature() to get detailed information about the parameters and return type of the process_data function. This information can be used to generate documentation, validate function calls, or adapt function behavior based on the provided arguments.
- Discovering Class Structure
  You can use inspect.getmembers() and other functions to explore the attributes and methods of a class, gaining insights into its design and capabilities.

```python
import inspect

class BaseClass:
```

```python
    base_attr = "Base"

    def base_method(self):
        pass

class MyClass(BaseClass):
    """My custom class."""
    class_attribute = 10

    def __init__(self, x, y):
        self.x = x
        self.y = y

    def my_method(self, z):
        """A method of MyClass."""
        return self.x + self.y + z

# Get all members of MyClass
members = inspect.getmembers(MyClass)
print("Members of MyClass:")
for name, value in members:
    print(f"  {name}: {value}")

# Get the methods of MyClass
methods = [
    name for name, value in inspect.getmembers(MyClass) if
inspect.isfunction(value)
]
print(f"\nMethods of MyClass: {methods}")
```

```
#Get the class hierarchy
print(inspect.getmro(MyClass))
```

- This example uses inspect.getmembers() to list all the attributes and methods of MyClass and its base classes. This helps in understanding the class's structure and how it interacts with its inheritance hierarchy.

## 3. Dynamic Behavior

- Dynamically Calling Functions
  By combining getattr() with information obtained from inspect, you can dynamically call functions or methods based on runtime conditions.

```python
import inspect

def add(x, y):
    return x + y

def subtract(x, y):
    return x - y

operations = {
    "add": add,
    "subtract": subtract,
}

def perform_operation(operation_name, a, b):
    """Performs an operation based on a string."""
```

```python
    operation_func = operations.get(operation_name)  # Get
function by name
  if operation_func:
     signature = inspect.signature(operation_func) #inspect the
signature
     try:
          bound_arguments = signature.bind(a,b) #bind the
arguments
              return operation_func(*bound_arguments.args,
**bound_arguments.kwargs)
     except TypeError as e:
        print(f"invalid arguments for {operation_name}")
        return None
  else:
     raise ValueError(f"Invalid operation: {operation_name}")


result1 = perform_operation("add", 5, 3)
print(result1)  # Output: 8

result2 = perform_operation("subtract", 10, 4)
print(result2)  # Output: 6

result3 = perform_operation("multiply", 2, 5)   # Raises
ValueError
```

- Here, the perform_operation function uses getattr() to dynamically retrieve the appropriate function based on the operation_name string. The inspect.signature is used to ensure that the correct arguments are passed. This allows for a very flexible way to execute different operations at runtime.

- Creating Adaptable Class Factories
  Metaclasses and inspect can be combined to create class factories that dynamically generate classes based on external data, such as configuration files or API responses.

```python
import inspect

class DynamicClassFactory(type):
    """A metaclass that creates classes dynamically from a specification."""

    def __new__(cls, name, bases, dct, spec):
        """Creates a new class based on the given specification."""
        if not isinstance(spec, dict):
            raise TypeError("Specification must be a dictionary")

        for key, value_type in spec.items():
            if not isinstance(value_type, type):
                raise TypeError(f"Value type for {key} must be a type")
            dct[key] = None  # Create attributes with default value None

    def __init__(self, **kwargs):
        """Dynamically generated __init__ method."""
        for key, value in kwargs.items():
```

```python
        if key not in spec:
            raise TypeError(f"Invalid argument: {key}")
        if not isinstance(value, spec[key]):
            raise TypeError(f"Argument {key} must be of
type {spec[key].__name__}")
        setattr(self, key, value)

    dct["__init__"] = __init__
    return super().__new__(cls, name, bases, dct)

def create_dynamic_class(name, spec):
    """Creates a dynamic class with a given specification."""
    return DynamicClassFactory(name, (object,), {}, spec=spec)

# Example usage:
user_spec = {
    "name": str,
    "age": int,
    "email": str,
}
User = create_dynamic_class("User", user_spec)   # Create
class

user1      =        User(name="Alice",        age=30,
email="alice@example.com") # Create instance
print(user1.name, user1.age, user1.email)

try:
        user2  =  User(name="Bob",  age="wrong",
email="bob@example.com") #error
```

```
except TypeError as e:
    print(e)
```

- In this example, the DynamicClassFactory metaclass uses a specification (a dictionary of attribute names and types) to dynamically create a class. The __init__ method is also dynamically generated to enforce the specified types. This demonstrates how metaprogramming with inspect can create highly adaptable classes.

# *CHAPTER 3*

# *Dynamic Code Execution with exec() and eval()*

*Fundamentals of Dynamic Code Execution in Python*

Dynamic code execution refers to the ability to execute code at runtime. This means that instead of code being set in stone when you write your program, you can create or modify it while the program is running. This capability is a cornerstone of Python's flexibility and allows for the creation of highly adaptable and extensible applications.

## 1. Core Concepts

- **Runtime vs. Compile Time:**
  - **Compile Time:** In languages like C++ or Java, code is typically compiled into machine code before the program is run. Any changes to the code require recompilation.
  - **Runtime:** Python is an interpreted language. This means that the interpreter reads and executes the code line by line as the program runs. Dynamic code execution happens during this runtime phase.
- **Code as Data:** A key concept in dynamic code execution is that code can be treated as data. This allows

you to manipulate code in the same way you would manipulate any other data type, such as strings or lists.
- **Dynamic Code Generation:** This involves constructing code (usually as a string) and then executing it. The code to be executed doesn't exist in the program's source code files but is created during the program's execution.

## 2. Techniques for Dynamic Code Execution in Python

Python provides several built-in functions and mechanisms for dynamic code execution:

- exec(object[, globals[, locals]])
    - The exec() function executes a block of Python code.
    - The code can be provided as a string, a code object, or a file object.
    - exec() is more general-purpose than eval() as it can handle multi-statement code, including function and class definitions, control flow statements, and more.
    - It does not return the result of the execution.
    - Example:

```python
code_string = """
def greet(name):
    print(f"Hello, {name}!")

greet("Python")
"""  # A multi-line string containing Python code
exec(code_string) # Execute the code defined in the string
```

- eval(expression[, globals[, locals]])
  - The eval() function evaluates a single Python expression.
  - It takes a string containing a valid Python expression as an argument.
  - It returns the result of the evaluated expression.
  - It is more limited than exec() and cannot execute statements like loops, function definitions, or class definitions.
  - Example:

```
expression = "2 + 3 * 4"
result = eval(expression)
print(result)  # Output: 14
```

- compile(source, filename, mode, flags=0, dont_inherit=False, optimize=-1, *, _feature_version=sys.version_info)
  * The compile function compiles the source string into a code object which can be executed by the functions exec() and eval().
  * The arguments source is the source code, normal string, a byte string, or an AST object.
  * The argument filename is the name of the file from which the code was read; if it wasn't read from a file, you can give a name yourself.
  * The argument mode is used to specify what kind of code the source represents; it can be 'exec' if source consists of a sequence of statements, 'eval' if it consists of a single expression, or 'single' if it consists of a single

interactive statement (in which case the value of the expression statement that is not None will be printed).

* Example:
```python
code_string = "x = 10\ny = 20\nresult = x + y\n"
compiled_code = compile(code_string, "<string>", "exec")
exec(compiled_code)
print(result)
```

●

● importlib.import_module(name, package=None)
   ○ This function dynamically imports a module by its name.
   ○ This allows you to load and use modules that were not known when the program started.
   ○ Example:

```
import importlib

module_name = "math"  # The name of the module to import
math_module = importlib.import_module(module_name)  # Import the module
print(math_module.sqrt(25))   # Use a function from the imported module
```
   ○

● **Metaclasses**
   ○ Metaclasses allow you to control the creation of classes.

- By defining a custom metaclass, you can dynamically modify class behavior or structure during class creation.
- This is a more advanced technique, and we will cover it in Chapter 5: The Magic of Metaclasses: Controlling Class Creation.

- Decorators
  * Decorators are a way to modify functions or classes.
  * They can be applied to a function or class using the @ symbol.
  * Decorators can dynamically add functionality.
  * We'll explore this in Chapter 4: Mastering Code Modification with Decorators.

## 3. Use Cases and Benefits

Dynamic code execution offers several advantages:

- **Extensibility:**
  - It allows you to create applications that can be extended with new functionality at runtime.
  - For example, you can design a plugin system where users can add new features by providing Python scripts. The application can then dynamically load and execute these scripts.
- **Adaptability:**
  - It enables programs to adapt to changing conditions or user input.
  - For instance, you can create an application that can process different data formats by dynamically generating code to handle each format.

- **Configuration:**
  - You can use dynamic code execution to load and execute code from configuration files.
  - This allows you to change the behavior of your application without modifying its core code.
- **Domain-Specific Languages (DSLs):**
  - Dynamic code execution can be used to create DSLs, which are specialized languages tailored to a particular problem domain.
  - You can define the syntax and semantics of your DSL and then use exec() or eval() to execute code written in that language.

## 4. Security Considerations

- **Code Injection Vulnerabilities:** A critical consideration with dynamic code execution is security. If you allow your program to execute arbitrary code from untrusted sources (e.g., user input, network requests), you create a security vulnerability. An attacker could inject malicious code that could harm your system.
- **Mitigation Strategies:**
  - **Never execute untrusted code:** The most important rule is to avoid executing code from sources you don't control.
  - **Restrict the execution environment:** Use the globals and locals parameters of exec() and eval() to limit the scope of the executed code and prevent it from accessing sensitive resources.

o Use the ast module: For more complex code manipulation, use the ast (Abstract Syntax Tree) module to parse and analyze code before execution. This allows you to validate the code's structure and ensure it doesn't contain any harmful operations.

o **Principle of Least Privilege:** Grant the code being executed the minimum necessary permissions.

## 5. Best Practices

- **Use dynamic code execution judiciously:** It adds complexity and potential security risks, so use it only when necessary.
- **Prioritize security:** Always be aware of the security implications and take appropriate precautions.
- **Keep code clear and maintainable:** Write your dynamically generated code in a way that is easy to understand and debug.
- **Document your code:** Clearly explain why you are using dynamic code execution and how it works.

*Using the exec() Statement for Executing Code Snippets and Strings*

The exec() function is a powerful tool in Python that allows you to execute arbitrary Python code dynamically. This means you can construct code as a string or a compiled code object and then have the Python interpreter run that code during the program's execution.

1. The Basics of exec()

- **Functionality:** The exec() function executes a block of Python code. This code can be:
    - A string containing Python statements.
    - A code object (e.g., created by the compile() function).
- **Syntax:**

exec(object[, globals[, locals]])

    - object: The code to execute (string or code object).
    - globals (optional): A dictionary representing the global namespace in which the code is executed.
    - locals (optional): A mapping object (usually a dictionary) representing the local namespace.
- **Execution Context:** When exec() is called, the provided code is executed within a specific context defined by the globals and locals dictionaries. These dictionaries provide the names and values that are accessible to the code being executed. If these are not provided, the current global and local namespaces are used.
- **Return Value:** exec() always returns None. Its purpose is to execute code for its side effects (e.g., modifying variables, printing output), not to return a value.

2. Executing Code Snippets and Strings

- **Simple Example:**

```
code_string = "print('Hello from exec()!')"
exec(code_string)  # Output: Hello from exec()!
```

In this case, exec() executes a simple print statement.

- **Multi-Statement Example:**

```
code_string = """
x = 10
y = 20
result = x + y
print(f"The sum of {x} and {y} is {result}")
"""
exec(code_string)  # Output: The sum of 10 and 20 is 30
```
```exec()``` can handle multiple statements, including variable assignments and calculations.

- **Defining Functions and Classes:**

```
code_string = """
def greet(name):
    return f"Hello, {name}!"

class Calculator:
    def add(self, x, y):
        return x + y

my_calc = Calculator()
print(my_calc.add(5, 3))
print(greet("World"))
"""
exec(code_string)
```
```

```
# Output: 8
#        Hello, World!
```

- You can even define functions and classes dynamically using exec().

## 3. Applications in Adaptable and Extensible Systems

The ability to execute code dynamically with exec() has significant implications for building adaptable and extensible applications:

- **Plugin Systems:**
    - exec() allows you to create applications where new functionality can be added at runtime through plugins.
    - Plugins can be distributed as separate files or modules containing Python code.
    - The main application can then dynamically load and execute these plugins using exec(), effectively extending its capabilities without modifying its core code.
    - Example:

```python
import os
import importlib

plugin_dir = "plugins"  # Directory where plugins are stored

def load_plugins():
    """Loads plugins from a directory."""
    for filename in os.listdir(plugin_dir):
```

```python
    if filename.endswith(".py"):
        module_name = filename[:-3]  # Remove ".py" extension
        try:
            # Attempt to import the module dynamically
            spec = importlib.util.spec_from_file_location(module_name, os.path.join(plugin_dir, filename))
            module = importlib.util.module_from_spec(spec)
            spec.loader.exec_module(module)
            #The module is loaded and executed and now can be used
            if hasattr(module, "register"):
                module.register()  # Register the plugin with the application
            print(f"Loaded plugin: {module_name}")
        except Exception as e:
            print(f"Failed to load plugin {module_name}: {e}")

# Example plugin (plugins/my_plugin.py):
"""
def register():
    print("My Plugin is registered")
"""

load_plugins()  # Load and register plugins
```

- **Dynamic Configuration:**

- Instead of hardcoding application behavior, you can store configuration information as Python code in external files or databases.
- The application can then use exec() to execute this configuration code at runtime, allowing you to change the application's behavior without modifying its source code.
- Example:

```
config_string = """
# Application configuration
log_level = "INFO"
max_connections = 100
feature_flags = {
    "enable_new_feature": True,
    "use_dark_mode": False,
}
"""

config = {}  # Dictionary to store configuration
exec(config_string, {}, config)  # Execute config code in the
config dictionary


# Access configuration values
print(config["log_level"])
print(config["max_connections"])
print(config["feature_flags"])
```

- **Adaptable Data Processing:**
  - You can use exec() to generate code that processes data in different formats or with varying structures.

- This is useful when dealing with data from external sources that may not have a consistent schema.
- Example:

```python
def process_data(data, data_format):
    """Processes data dynamically based on the format."""
    if data_format == "csv":
        code_string = """
def process(data):
    for row in data.splitlines():
        values = row.split(",")
        # process the values
        print(f"Processed row: {values}")
        # print(row)
"""
        exec(code_string)
    elif data_format == "json":
        code_string = """
import json
def process(data):
    parsed_data = json.loads(data)
    # process the parsed data
    print(f"processed json data {parsed_data}")
"""
        exec(code_string)
    else:
        raise ValueError(f"Unsupported data format: {data_format}")
    process(data)
```

```
csv_data        =        "name,age,city\nAlice,30,New
York\nBob,25,London"
json_data = '{"name": "Charlie", "age": 35, "city": "Paris"}'

process_data(csv_data, "csv")
process_data(json_data, "json")
```

## *Evaluating Expressions Dynamically with Python's eval() Function*

The eval() function in Python provides a way to evaluate Python expressions dynamically. While exec() executes blocks of code, eval() is specifically designed for evaluating single expressions. This makes it a powerful tool for certain use cases, such as dynamic configuration and adaptable logic.

## 1. Understanding eval()

- **Functionality:** The eval() function evaluates a string as a Python expression.
- **Expression:** An expression is a piece of code that produces a value. Examples of expressions include:
  - Arithmetic operations: $2 + 3$, $x * 5$
  - Variable lookups: my_variable
  - Function calls: max(1, 2)
  - Logical operations: True and False
- **Syntax:**
eval(expression[, globals[, locals]])

  - expression: The string containing the Python expression to be evaluated.

- o globals (optional): A dictionary representing the global namespace.
- o locals (optional): A mapping object (usually a dictionary) representing the local namespace.
- **Evaluation Context:** Similar to exec(), eval() evaluates the expression within a specific context defined by the globals and locals dictionaries. These dictionaries determine which names (variables, functions) are accessible during the evaluation. If not provided, the current global and local namespaces are used.
- **Return Value:** Unlike exec(), eval() returns the result of the evaluated expression.

## 2. Key Differences Between eval() and exec()

| Feature | eval() | exec() |
|---------|--------|--------|
| Purpose | Evaluates a single expression. | Executes a block of code (statements). |
| Input | String containing a single Python expression. | String or code object containing Python code (statements, functions, classes, etc.). |

| Return Value | Returns the result of the expression. | Returns None. |
|---|---|---|
| Use Cases | Evaluating calculations, dynamic logic, limited configuration. | Executing code snippets, defining functions/classes, plugin systems, more complex configuration. |
| Security Risk | Potentially less risky if used carefully (only expressions are allowed). | Generally considered riskier due to the ability to execute arbitrary code. |

## 3. Using eval() for Adaptable Logic

eval() can be employed to create code that adapts its behavior based on dynamically computed expressions.

- **Example: Dynamic Calculation**

```
def calculate(operation, x, y):

    """

    Performs a calculation based on a string expression.
```

```python
    """
    expression = f"{x} {operation} {y}"

    try:

        result = eval(expression)

        return result

    except Exception as e:

        return f"Error: Invalid operation - {e}"

print(calculate("+", 5, 3))  # Output: 8

print(calculate("*", 2, 4))  # Output: 8

print(calculate("/", 10, 2))  # Output: 5.0

print(calculate("**", 2, 3))  # Output: 8

print(calculate("invalid", 2, 3))   # Output: Error: Invalid
operation - name 'invalid' is not defined
```

In this example, the calculate function takes an operator as a string and uses eval() to dynamically construct and evaluate an arithmetic expression. This allows the function to perform different calculations without needing a series of if/elif statements.

- **Example: Conditional Logic from String**

```python
def check_condition(condition, context):

    """
```

Checks a boolean condition dynamically, with access to a limited context.

```python
    """

    try:

        result = eval(condition, {}, context)  # Pass in specific context

        return bool(result)  # Ensure a boolean result

    except Exception as e:

        print(f"Error evaluating condition: {e}")

        return False  # Default to False on error

# Define a limited context with allowed variables

my_context = {

    "age": 25,

    "name": "Alice",

    "is_adult": True,

}

condition1 = "age > 18 and is_adult"

condition2 = "name == 'Bob'"

condition3 = "city == 'London'"  # this variable is not in the context
```

```python
print(check_condition(condition1, my_context))    # Output:
True

print(check_condition(condition2, my_context))    # Output:
False

print(check_condition(condition3, my_context))    # Output:
Error evaluating condition: name 'city' is not defined,  False
```

- Here, the check_condition function evaluates a boolean expression provided as a string. The variables accessible to the expression are controlled by the context dictionary, making it safer.

### 4. Using eval() for Dynamic Configuration

eval() can be used to load configuration values from strings, allowing for more flexible and expressive configuration than simple key-value pairs.

- **Example: Evaluating Configuration Expressions**

```python
config_string = """

{

  "log_level": "INFO",

  "timeout": 10 * 2,  # Evaluate an expression for timeout

  "retry_strategy": {

    "max_retries": 3,
```

```python
    "delay": [1, 2, 4, 8]  # A list defined as part of the config
    },

    "use_feature_x": True if 1+1 == 2 else False,  # Conditional
assignment
}
"""

# Use a safe context, limiting available names to None
config_data = eval(config_string, {"__builtins__": {}})
print(config_data)
# Output:
# {
#     'log_level': 'INFO',
#     'timeout': 20,
#     'retry_strategy': {'max_retries': 3, 'delay': [1, 2, 4, 8]},
#     'use_feature_x': True
# }
print(f"Log Level: {config_data['log_level']}")
print(f"Timeout: {config_data['timeout']}")
print(f"Retry Delay: {config_data['retry_strategy']['delay']}")
```

```
print(f"Feature X: {config_data['use_feature_x']}")
```

- In this example, eval() parses a string containing a dictionary with configuration values. The values can be simple strings or more complex expressions. This allows you to define configuration settings with a more Pythonic syntax and even include simple logic.

## 5. Security Considerations with eval()

- **The Risk of Arbitrary Code Execution:** The primary danger with eval() is that it can execute arbitrary Python code if the expression being evaluated comes from an untrusted source (e.g., user input). This can lead to serious security vulnerabilities.
- **Mitigating Risks:**
  - Never use eval() with untrusted input: This is the most important rule. If you cannot guarantee that the expression is safe, do not use eval().
  - **Control the execution environment:** The globals and locals arguments can be used to restrict the names that are available to the expression being evaluated. This is crucial for security.
- **Safer Alternatives:**
  - For simple calculations, use a safe parser or write your own expression evaluator.
  - For more complex logic, consider using a Domain-Specific Language (DSL) and a dedicated parser.

- If you need to deserialize data, use formats like JSON or YAML with their respective safe loading functions (e.g., json.loads(), yaml.safe_load()).

## 6. Best Practices

- Use eval() sparingly: Prefer safer alternatives whenever possible.
- **Sanitize input:** If you must use eval() with input from a potentially untrusted source, sanitize the input to remove any potentially dangerous code. This is extremely difficult to do reliably.
- **Restrict namespaces:** Always pass in carefully constructed globals and locals dictionaries to limit the scope of execution and prevent access to sensitive names.
- **Document your code:** Clearly explain why you are using eval() and what security measures you have taken.

## *Understanding Namespaces and Scope in Dynamic Code Execution*

When you execute code dynamically using functions like exec() or eval(), it's crucial to understand how namespaces and scope affect the execution. This knowledge is essential for maintaining control over the code's behavior, preventing unintended side effects, and ensuring both efficiency and predictability.

## 1. Namespaces

- **Definition:** A namespace is a collection of names (identifiers) that are mapped to corresponding objects (variables, functions, classes, etc.). Think of it as a dictionary where the keys are the names and the values are the objects they refer to.
- **Types of Namespaces:** Python has several types of namespaces:
  - **Built-in Namespace:** Contains names that are always available in Python (e.g., len, print, True).
  - **Global Namespace:** Contains names defined at the module level (i.e., outside of any function or class).
  - **Local Namespace:** Contains names defined within a function.
  - **Enclosing Namespace:** Exists in nested functions, where an inner function can access names from the outer function's scope.
- **Importance:** Namespaces prevent name collisions. The same name can refer to different objects in different namespaces. For example, a variable named x inside a function is different from a variable named x at the module level.

## 2. Scope

- **Definition:** Scope refers to the region of a program where a particular name is accessible. It determines the visibility of a name.
- **LEGB Rule:** Python uses the LEGB rule to determine the order in which namespaces are searched:

- Local: Names in the current function's namespace.
- Enclosing: Names in the namespaces of any enclosing functions.
- Global: Names in the module's namespace.
- Built-in: Names in the built-in namespace.

- **Example:**

```
global_var = 10  # Global variable

def outer_function():
    outer_var = 20  # Enclosing variable

    def inner_function():
        local_var = 30 # Local variable
        print(f"Local: {local_var}")        # Accessing local variable
        print(f"Enclosing: {outer_var}")        # Accessing enclosing variable
        print(f"Global: {global_var}")        # Accessing global variable
        print(f"Built-in: {len([1,2,3])}")  # Accessing built-in function

    inner_function()

outer_function()
```

## 3. Dynamic Code Execution and Namespaces

When you use exec() or eval(), you introduce a new execution context, and the way namespaces are handled becomes critical.

- **Default Behavior:**
  If you don't provide the optional globals and locals arguments to exec() or eval(), the code is executed in the current scope. This means it can access and modify variables in the current global and local namespaces. This is generally dangerous.
- **Controlling the Execution Context:**
  The globals and locals arguments allow you to control the namespaces that are accessible to the dynamically executed code.
  - globals: Provides a dictionary that serves as the global namespace for the executed code. It must be a dictionary.
  - locals: Provides a mapping object (usually a dictionary) that serves as the local namespace. It can be any mapping type.
- **Why Control is Important:**
  - **Security:** If you execute untrusted code with exec() or eval(), you must restrict its access to your program's variables and functions. By providing carefully constructed globals and locals dictionaries, you can prevent the code from accessing or modifying sensitive data or executing harmful operations.
  - **Predictability:** Controlling namespaces makes the behavior of your dynamically executed code more predictable. You can ensure that it has access to only the names you intend it to have,

preventing unexpected side effects or dependencies on the surrounding code.

- ○ **Isolation:** Using separate namespaces helps to isolate the dynamically executed code from the rest of your program, reducing the risk of conflicts and making your code more modular.
- ○ **Efficiency:** By providing a limited namespace, you can sometimes improve performance, as the interpreter doesn't have to search through as many scopes to resolve names.

4. Best Practices for Using exec() and eval() with Namespaces

- **Use Separate Namespaces:** Always provide explicit globals and locals dictionaries when using exec() or eval(). Avoid relying on the default behavior of executing in the current scope.
- Restrict globals: For maximum security, provide a minimal globals dictionary, ideally containing only the __builtins__ dictionary with its standard built-in names, and even that can be restricted.
- Control locals: The locals dictionary should contain only the names that the executed code is explicitly allowed to access. This might include specific variables or functions that you intend to expose.
- **Example: Safe Execution with Restricted Namespaces**

```
def safe_execute(code_string, allowed_names):
    """
    Executes a code string in a restricted environment.
```

```python
    """
    # Create a restricted globals dictionary
    safe_globals = {
        "__builtins__": {
            "True": True,
            "False": False,
            "None": None,
            "int": int,
            "float": float,
            "str": str,
            "bool": bool,
            "list": list,
            "dict": dict,
            "tuple": tuple,
            "set": set,
            "len": len,
            "max": max,
            "min": min,
            "abs": abs,
            "print": __builtins__["print"], # Allow print,
        }
    } # Include only essential built-ins

    # Create a restricted locals dictionary with allowed names
        safe_locals = {name: value for name, value in
allowed_names.items()}

    try:
        exec(code_string, safe_globals, safe_locals)
    except Exception as e:
```

```python
        print(f"Error executing code: {e}")
        return None  # Or handle the error as appropriate


# Example usage:
user_code = "result = x + y; print(result)"  # Code from a user
(potentially untrusted)
allowed_vars = {"x": 5, "y": 10}  # Define allowed variables


safe_execute(user_code, allowed_vars)  # Output: 15


# Example of unsafe code
user_code_unsafe = "import os; os.system('rm -rf /')"  #
Dangerous code
safe_execute(user_code_unsafe, allowed_vars)  # Error: Name
'os' is not defined
```

### *Security Considerations and Best Practices for Using exec() and eval()*

The exec() and eval() functions in Python offer powerful capabilities for dynamic code execution, but they also introduce significant security risks if not used carefully. Since they allow the execution of arbitrary code at runtime, they can be exploited to inject malicious code into your application. This section delves into the security implications of using these functions and provides best practices to mitigate those risks.

**1. The Dangers of Uncontrolled Code Execution**

- **Code Injection:** The primary security risk is code injection. If the input to exec() or eval() comes from an untrusted source (e.g., user input, network requests, external files), an attacker can insert malicious code into that input. This code will then be executed with the same privileges as your Python program.

- **Potential Damage:** The consequences of code injection can be severe, including:
  - **Data Breaches:** Attackers can gain access to sensitive data, such as passwords, API keys, or personal information.
  - **System Compromise:** They can execute system commands, modify files, or even take complete control of the server.
  - **Denial of Service:** They can crash your application or make it unavailable to legitimate users.
- **Principle of Least Privilege:** The core security principle at play here is the Principle of Least Privilege. Code should only have the minimum necessary privileges to function correctly. exec() and eval(), by their nature, can violate this principle by allowing the execution of code with the privileges of the calling program.

## 2. Understanding the Attack Surface

To effectively mitigate the risks, it's crucial to understand the attack surface:

- **Untrusted Input:** The most dangerous scenario is when the input for exec() or eval() comes from an untrusted source. This could be:
    - **User Input:** Data entered by a user through a form, command-line interface, or other input method.
    - **Network Requests:** Data received from a remote server or API.
    - **External Files:** Code loaded from a file that might be modified by an attacker.
    - **Database Queries:** Code retrieved from a database that could be manipulated.
- **The Scope of Execution:** The code executed by exec() and eval() has access to the namespaces in which it runs. This means it can potentially access and modify variables, functions, and objects defined in those namespaces.

## 3. Mitigation Strategies: Best Practices

The following are essential best practices to minimize the security risks associated with exec() and eval():

- **Never Execute Untrusted Code:** The most crucial rule is: *never* use exec() or eval() with input from an untrusted source. If you cannot guarantee the safety of the code you are executing, do not use these functions.
- **Restrict the Execution Environment:**
    - Use the globals and locals Parameters: Both exec() and eval() accept optional globals and

locals arguments, which allow you to specify the namespaces in which the code will be executed. Always use these parameters to create a restricted execution environment.

- ○ **Control the Global Namespace:**
  - ■ The globals parameter should be a dictionary.
  - ■ For maximum security, start with an empty dictionary or a dictionary containing only the __builtins__ dictionary with a safe subset of built-in functions.
  - ■ Completely removing the __builtins__ dictionary is not recommended, as it can break even seemingly harmless code (e.g., code that uses len() or print()). A safer approach is to restrict it.
- ○ **Control the Local Namespace:**
  - ■ The locals parameter should be a mapping object (usually a dictionary).
  - ■ It should contain only the variables and functions that the executed code is explicitly allowed to access.
  - ■ This allows you to provide a limited interface to the code being executed, preventing it from accessing other parts of your program.
- • **Example: Safe Execution with Restricted Namespaces**

```
def safe_eval(expression, allowed_names):
    """
```

Evaluates an expression in a restricted environment.
"""

```python
# Create a safe globals dictionary
safe_globals = {
    '__builtins__': {
        'True': True,
        'False': False,
        'None': None,
        'int': int,
        'float': float,
        'str': str,
        'bool': bool,
        'list': list,
        'dict': dict,
        'tuple': tuple,
        'set': set,
        'len': len,
        'max': max,
        'min': min,
        'abs': abs,
        'print': __builtins__['print'], # Allow print,
    }
} # Include only essential built-ins

# Create a safe locals dictionary with allowed names
safe_locals = {name: value for name, value in allowed_names.items()}

try:
    result = eval(expression, safe_globals, safe_locals)
```

```python
        return result
    except Exception as e:
        print(f"Error evaluating expression: {e}")
        return None  # Or raise a custom exception


# Example usage
safe_expression1 = "x + y"
allowed_vars1 = {"x": 5, "y": 10}
result1 = safe_eval(safe_expression1, allowed_vars1)
print(result1)  # Output: 15


safe_expression2 = "z * 2"  # z is not in allowed_vars2
allowed_vars2 = {"x": 5, "y": 10}
result2 = safe_eval(safe_expression2, allowed_vars2)
print(result2)  # Output: Error evaluating expression: name 'z'
is not defined, None


safe_expression3 = "__import__('os').system('ls -l')"  #
Dangerous code
allowed_vars3 = {"x": 5, "y": 10}
result3 = safe_eval(safe_expression3, allowed_vars2)
print(result3)  # will throw an error
```

- **Use Abstract Syntax Trees (ASTs) for Code Analysis:**
  For more complex scenarios where you need to analyze
  or modify code before execution, use the ast module to
  work with Abstract Syntax Trees. This allows you to
  inspect the code's structure and ensure it doesn't contain
  any prohibited constructs before it is executed. This is a

more advanced technique, but it provides a much higher level of security than simply trying to sanitize strings.

- **Avoid Dynamic Code Generation When Possible:**
  If you can achieve the desired functionality through safer means, such as using data structures, functions, or object-oriented programming, do so. Dynamic code generation should be used only when it is truly necessary for adaptability or extensibility.

- **Document Security Measures:**
  If you must use exec() or eval(), document your code thoroughly. Clearly explain the security risks involved and the steps you have taken to mitigate them. This will help other developers (and your future self) understand the code and avoid introducing new vulnerabilities.

# *CHAPTER 4*

# *Mastering Code Modification with Decorators*

---

*Introduction to Decorators: Enhancing Functions and Methods*

Decorators are a powerful and elegant feature in Python that allows you to modify or extend the behavior of functions and methods without changing their actual code. They provide a concise and readable way to add functionality such as logging, memoization, authentication, or input validation to your existing functions or methods.

## 1. Understanding Decorators

- Functions as First-Class Objects: In Python, functions are treated as first-class objects. This means you can:
    - Assign them to variables
    - Pass them as arguments to other functions
    - Return them as values from other functions
- Decorator Function: A decorator is essentially a function that takes another function as an argument, wraps it in a closure, and returns the wrapped function.
- The @ Syntax: The @ symbol is syntactic sugar for applying a decorator to a function.
    - Example:

```python
def my_decorator(func):
    def wrapper():
        print("Something before...")
        func()
        print("Something after...")
    return wrapper

@my_decorator
def say_hello():
    print("Hello!")

say_hello()
```

- o In this example, @my_decorator is equivalent to say_hello = my_decorator(say_hello).
- Wrapping: Decorators wrap the original function, replacing it with a modified version. The wrapper function typically contains the original function call, along with any added functionality.

## 2. How Decorators Work

A decorator function typically defines an inner function called a "wrapper". This wrapper function does the following:

1. Executes any pre-processing steps (e.g., logging, authentication).
2. Calls the original function, passing any arguments it received.
3. Executes any post-processing steps (e.g., logging, modifying the result).

4. Returns the result of the original function (or a modified version of it).

The decorator function then returns this wrapper function. When you call the original function, you're actually calling the wrapper.

## 3. Benefits of Using Decorators

- Code Reusability: Decorators allow you to define a piece of functionality once and apply it to multiple functions or methods. This promotes code reuse and reduces redundancy.
- Readability: They make your code more readable by separating the core logic of your functions from the additional functionality.
- Clean Code: Decorators help to keep your code clean and organized by avoiding the need to modify the original functions directly.
- Separation of Concerns: They promote a cleaner design by separating different concerns. For example, logging or authentication logic is kept separate from the business logic of your functions.
- Extensibility: They provide an easy way to extend the behavior of functions and methods without altering their definitions.

### *Function Decorators in Python*

Function decorators are a powerful feature that allows you to enhance or modify the behavior of functions or methods without altering their underlying code structure. They provide a clean and Pythonic way to implement cross-cutting concerns, promoting code reuse and improving readability.

## 1. What is a Function Decorator?

- A decorator is a function that takes another function as an argument.
- It extends or modifies the behavior of the argument function.
- It returns a new function (usually a wrapper function) that incorporates the modified behavior.
- The original function is replaced by this new, decorated function.

## 2. Decorator Syntax

Python provides a special syntax using the @ symbol to apply decorators:

```python
def my_decorator(func):
    def wrapper(*args, **kwargs):
        # Code to be executed before the original function
        print("Executing before the function...")
        result = func(*args, **kwargs)  # Call the original function
        # Code to be executed after the original function
        print("Executing after the function...")
        return result
    return wrapper
```

```
@my_decorator
def my_function(x):
    print(f"Inside my_function({x})")
    return x * 2


my_function(5)
```

In this example, @my_decorator decorates my_function. When my_function(5) is called:

1. The my_decorator function is called with my_function as an argument.
2. my_decorator returns the wrapper function.
3. my_function is replaced by the wrapper function.
4. The code within the wrapper is executed, which includes the call to the original my_function.

## 3. How Function Decorators Work

Let's break down how function decorators work step by step:

1. Define the Decorator Function:
   - It takes a function (func) as input.
   - It usually defines a nested function (the wrapper) that will replace the original function.
   - The wrapper function can execute code before and/or after calling the original function.
   - The decorator function returns the wrapper function.
2. Apply the Decorator:

- The @decorator_name syntax is used before the function definition you want to decorate.
- This is syntactic sugar for: my_function = my_decorator(my_function)

3. Function Call:
- When you call the decorated function (my_function in the example), you are actually calling the wrapper function returned by the decorator.
- The wrapper executes its added code and then calls the original function (if needed).

**4. Preserving Function Metadata with functools.wraps**

When a function is decorated, the wrapper function replaces the original function. This can change the original function's metadata, such as its name and docstring. To preserve this information, you should use the @functools.wraps decorator.

```python
import functools

def my_decorator(func):
    @functools.wraps(func)  # Preserves original function's metadata
    def wrapper(*args, **kwargs):
        """Wrapper function for my_decorator."""
        print("Executing before...")
        result = func(*args, **kwargs)
        print("Executing after...")
        return result
    return wrapper
```

```python
@my_decorator
def my_function(x):
    """My original function."""
    print(f"Inside my_function({x})")
    return x * 2

print(my_function.__name__)  # Output: my_function (instead of 'wrapper')
print(my_function.__doc__)  # Output: My original function.
```

5. Common Use Cases for Function Decorators

- Logging: Decorators can be used to log function calls, arguments, execution time, and return values.
- Timing: You can measure the execution time of functions using decorators.
- Authentication and Authorization: Decorators can check if a user is authenticated or has the necessary permissions to access a function.
- Input Validation: Decorators can validate the arguments passed to a function before it is executed.
- Caching (Memoization): Decorators can cache the results of expensive function calls to improve performance.
- Retry Mechanism: Decorators can be used to retry a function call if it fails.
- Transaction Management: Decorators can manage database transactions, ensuring that a function's operations are performed atomically.

6. Benefits of Function Decorators

- Code Reusability: Decorators promote code reuse by allowing you to apply the same functionality to multiple functions without rewriting it.
- Improved Readability: They make your code more readable by separating concerns and keeping the core logic of your functions clean.
- Modularity: Decorators help to create more modular code, where different aspects of functionality are handled independently.
- Maintainability: They make your code easier to maintain by reducing code duplication and making it easier to modify or extend functionality.

*Class Decorators in Python*

While function decorators modify the behavior of functions or methods, class decorators allow you to modify the behavior of an entire class. This opens up powerful possibilities for altering class definitions at runtime.

**1. What is a Class Decorator?**

- A class decorator is a class or function that takes a class as an argument.
- It modifies that class in some way.
- It returns the original class or a modified version of it.
- They are applied using the @ syntax, just like function decorators.

**2. How Class Decorators Work**

- **Basic Mechanism:**
  1. The class decorator function is called with the class object as its argument.
  2. The decorator function can then:
     - Modify the class's attributes (methods, variables).
     - Add new attributes.
     - Replace the original class with a different one.
  3. The modified class (or a new class) is then assigned back to the original class name.
- **Example:**

```python
def add_class_attribute(cls):

    cls.new_attribute = "Added by decorator"  # Add a new class attribute

    return cls

@add_class_attribute

class MyClass:

    existing_attribute = 10

print(MyClass.new_attribute)  # Output: Added by decorator
```

In this example, the add_class_attribute decorator adds a new attribute to MyClass.

## 3. Key Differences from Function Decorators

| Feature | Function Decorators | Class Decorators |
|---------|---------------------|------------------|
| Decorates | Functions or methods | Classes |
| Argument | A function or method object | A class object |
| Purpose | Modify the behavior of a specific function or method | Modify the behavior or attributes of an entire class |

## 4. Modifying Class Behavior and Attributes

Class decorators can be used to perform a variety of modifications to a class:

- **Adding Methods:** You can add new methods to a class.

```
def add_method(cls):
    def new_method(self):
        return f"This is a new method in {cls.__name__}"
    cls.new_method = new_method
    return cls
```

```python
@add_method
class MyClass:
    pass

obj = MyClass()
print(obj.new_method())  # Output: This is a new method in MyClass
```

- **Modifying Existing Methods:** You can replace or wrap existing methods to change their behavior.

```python
def modify_method(cls):

    original_init = cls.__init__  # Store the original __init__


    def new_init(self, *args, **kwargs):

        print(f"Initializing {cls.__name__} with {args}, {kwargs}")  # Enhanced initialization

        original_init(self, *args, **kwargs)  # Call the original __init__

        self.extra_attribute = "Extra"  # Add an extra attribute


    cls.__init__ = new_init  # Replace the original __init__

    return cls
```

```
@modify_method
class MyClass:
  def __init__(self, x, y):
    self.x = x
    self.y = y

obj = MyClass(1, 2)
print(obj.x, obj.y, obj.extra_attribute)  # Output: 1 2 Extra
```

- **Adding Attributes:** You can add new class or instance attributes.

```
def add_attributes(cls):

  cls.class_attribute = "New Class Attribute"  # Add a class
attribute

  def __init__(self, *args, **kwargs):

    super(cls, self).__init__(*args, **kwargs)

    self.instance_attribute = "New Instance Attribute"



  if hasattr(cls, '__init__'):

    old_init = cls.__init__

    def new_init(self, *args, **kwargs):

      old_init(self, *args, **kwargs)
      self.instance_attribute = "New Instance Attribute"
    cls.__init__ = new_init
```

```
  else:
    cls.__init__ = __init__
  return cls


@add_attributes
class MyClass:
  def __init__(self, a):
    self.a = a


print(MyClass.class_attribute)  # Output: New Class Attribute
obj = MyClass(10)
print(obj.instance_attribute)  # Output: New Instance Attribute
print(obj.a)
```

- **Enforcing Class Structure:** You can use class decorators to enforce specific requirements on a class, such as requiring certain methods or attributes to be defined.

```
def enforce_interface(cls):

  if not hasattr(cls, "required_method"):

      raise TypeError(f"Class {cls.__name__} must implement
'required_method'")

  return cls


@enforce_interface
class MyClass:
  def required_method(self):
    pass
```

```
# @enforce_interface
# class BadClass:  # Raises a TypeError at class definition time
#    pass
```

## 5. Benefits of Class Decorators

- **Modification at Definition Time:** Class decorators modify classes when they are defined, allowing you to alter their structure before any instances are created.
- **Centralized Modification:** They provide a centralized way to apply modifications to multiple classes, promoting consistency and reducing code duplication.
- **Metaprogramming Capabilities:** Class decorators enable powerful metaprogramming techniques, allowing you to manipulate classes in a very flexible way.
- **Adaptable Class Structures:** They make it possible to create adaptable class structures that can be modified based on configuration, environment, or other dynamic factors.

*Parameterized Decorators in Python*

Parameterized decorators are a powerful extension of the basic decorator concept, allowing you to create decorators that can accept arguments. This capability greatly enhances their flexibility and reusability, enabling you to customize their behavior to suit different situations.

## 1. The Structure of a Parameterized Decorator

A parameterized decorator involves an extra layer of function nesting:

1. **Decorator Factory:** This is an outer function that accepts the parameters you want to use in the decorator.
2. **Decorator Function:** This is a nested function within the decorator factory. It takes the function to be decorated as an argument.
3. **Wrapper Function:** This is a nested function within the decorator function. It wraps the original function and adds the desired behavior.

Here's a general structure:

```python
def decorator_factory(decorator_arguments):   # 1. Decorator Factory

    def decorator_function(func):        # 2. Decorator Function

        def wrapper_function(*args, **kwargs):  # 3. Wrapper Function

            # Code to be executed before the original function

            # ...

            result = func(*args, **kwargs)  # Call the original function

            # Code to be executed after the original function
            # ...
            return result
        return wrapper_function
    return decorator_function
```

## 2. Example: A Parameterized Retry Decorator

Let's create a decorator that retries a function a specified number of times:

```python
import time
from typing import Callable, TypeVar, ParamSpec, Any

P = ParamSpec('P')
R = TypeVar('R')

def retry(max_retries: int, delay: float = 1, exceptions:
type[Exception] | tuple[type[Exception], ...] = Exception) ->
Callable[[Callable[P, R]], Callable[P, R]]:
    """
    Retries a function with a specified number of times.
    :param max_retries: the maximum number of retries
    :param delay: the delay between retries in seconds
        :param exceptions: the exception or exceptions that will
trigger a retry

    """

    def decorator_function(func: Callable[P, R]) -> Callable[P,
R]:

        def wrapper_function(*args: P.args, **kwargs: P.kwargs)
-> R:
            attempts = 0
            while attempts < max_retries:
                try:
                    return func(*args, **kwargs)
                except exceptions as e:
```

```python
            attempts += 1
            print(f"Attempt {attempts} failed: {e}")
            if attempts < max_retries:
                time.sleep(delay)
            else:
                raise  # Re-raise the last exception
            return func(*args, **kwargs)  #this will never be
reached
    return wrapper_function
  return decorator_function


@retry(max_retries=3, delay=2, exceptions=(TimeoutError,
ConnectionError))
def fetch_data(url: str) -> str:

    """Fetches data from a URL, retrying on timeout or
connection errors."""

  print(f"Fetching data from {url}")

  # Simulate a timeout error on the first attempt

  if fetch_data.attempt_count < 1:

    fetch_data.attempt_count += 1

    raise TimeoutError("Simulated timeout error")
  else:
    return "Data from the URL"


fetch_data.attempt_count = 0
data = fetch_data("https://example.com/data")
```

```
print(data)
```

In this example:

- retry is the decorator factory. It takes max_retries, delay, and exceptions as arguments.
- It returns decorator_function.
- decorator_function takes the function to be decorated (func) as an argument and returns the wrapper_function.
- The @retry(max_retries=3, delay=2) syntax applies the decorator, effectively calling retry(max_retries=3, delay=2)(fetch_data).

## 3. Benefits of Parameterized Decorators

- **Flexibility:** Parameterized decorators provide a high degree of flexibility, allowing you to customize the decorator's behavior based on specific requirements.
- **Reusability:** They can be reused in various situations with different parameters, reducing code duplication.
- **Configuration:** They enable you to configure decorator behavior through parameters, making your code more adaptable to different environments or use cases.
- **Readability:** They can improve code readability by making the decorator's purpose and configuration clear at the point of use.

## 4. Common Use Cases

- **Customizable Logging:** You can create a parameterized logging decorator to log messages at different levels (e.g., DEBUG, INFO, ERROR) or to different destinations (e.g., console, file).

- **Flexible Authentication:** A parameterized authentication decorator can check for different roles or permissions, allowing you to control access to different parts of your application.
- **Smart Caching:** You can create a caching decorator where the cache's size, expiration time, or storage location can be configured using parameters.
- **Retry with Exponential Backoff:** A parameterized retry decorator can implement different retry strategies, such as exponential backoff, with configurable delay factors and maximum retry attempts.
- **Rate Limiting:** Decorators can be used to limit the number of requests a function can handle within a specific time window, and the parameters can define the rate limit and time window.

Parameterized decorators enhance code reuse and make your decorators more adaptable and extensible.


### *Advanced Decorator Techniques and Practical Applications*

Decorators are a powerful feature in Python, and mastering advanced techniques can significantly enhance your ability to write efficient and adaptable code. Here, we'll explore some of these advanced techniques and their practical applications.

### 1. Parameterized Decorators

As discussed previously, parameterized decorators enhance flexibility. Let's see some more advanced examples:

- **Example: Retry with Exponential Backoff**

```
import time
import random
from typing import Callable, TypeVar, ParamSpec, Any

P = ParamSpec('P')
R = TypeVar('R')

def retry_with_backoff(
    max_retries: int,
    initial_delay: float = 1,
    backoff_factor: float = 2,
    max_delay: float = 60,
    exceptions: type[Exception] | tuple[type[Exception], ...] =
Exception,
) -> Callable[[Callable[P, R]], Callable[P, R]]:
    """Retries a function with exponential backoff."""

    def decorator_function(func: Callable[P, R]) -> Callable[P,
R]:
        def wrapper_function(*args: P.args, **kwargs: P.kwargs)
-> R:
            attempts = 0
            delay = initial_delay
            while attempts < max_retries:
                try:
                    return func(*args, **kwargs)
                except exceptions as e:
```

```python
            attempts += 1
            print(f"Attempt {attempts} failed: {e}, retrying in {delay:.2f} seconds...")
            if attempts < max_retries:
                time.sleep(delay)
                delay = min(delay * backoff_factor, max_delay) # Exponential backoff with a maximum
            else:
                raise  # Re-raise the last exception
        return func(*args, **kwargs) #this will never be reached

    return wrapper_function

  return decorator_function

@retry_with_backoff(max_retries=5, initial_delay=0.5, backoff_factor=3, max_delay=10)
def unreliable_function(attempt: int) -> str:
    """Simulates an unreliable function that may raise an exception."""
    if random.random() < 0.3:  # Simulate a 30% failure rate
        raise ValueError(f"Simulated failure on attempt {attempt}")
    else:
        return "Success!"

for i in range(3):
    try:
        result = unreliable_function(i)
```

```
        print(f"Function call successful: {result}")
        break
    except Exception:
        Pass
```

- In this example, the retry_with_backoff decorator retries the decorated function with an exponential backoff strategy. The decorator factory takes parameters to configure the maximum number of retries, the initial delay, the backoff factor, the maximum delay, and the specific exceptions to catch. This makes the decorator highly reusable for various situations where retries are needed.

## 2. Decorating Classes

While decorators are commonly used with functions, they can also be applied to classes. A class decorator receives the class object as an argument and can modify it or replace it with another class.

- **Example: Adding Attributes and Methods to a Class**

```
def add_attributes_and_methods(cls):
    cls.new_attribute = "Added by decorator"  # Add a class attribute

    def new_method(self):
        return f"Hello from {cls.__name__}"  # Add an instance method

    cls.new_method = new_method
```

```python
    return cls

@add_attributes_and_methods
class MyClass:
    def __init__(self, x: int):
        self.x: int = x

obj = MyClass(10)
print(MyClass.new_attribute)  # Output: Added by decorator
print(obj.new_method())  # Output: Hello from MyClass
```

- Here, the add_attributes_and_methods decorator adds a class attribute and an instance method to the MyClass.
- **Example: Singleton Class Decorator**

```python
def singleton(cls):
    """A class decorator to create a singleton."""
    instances = {}

    def getinstance(*args: Any, **kwargs: Any) -> cls:
        if cls not in instances:
            instances[cls] = cls(*args, **kwargs)
        return instances[cls]

    return getinstance

@singleton
class DatabaseConnection:
    def __init__(self, host: str, port: int):
        self.host: str = host
        self.port: int = port
```

```
    print(f"Connecting to database at {self.host}:{self.port}")

db1 = DatabaseConnection("localhost", 5432)
db2 = DatabaseConnection("localhost", 5432)   # This will
return the same instance as db1

print(db1 is db2)  # Output: True
```

- This decorator ensures that only one instance of the DatabaseConnection class is ever created.

## 3. Decorator Composition (Stacking Decorators)

You can apply multiple decorators to a single function or class by stacking them. The decorators are applied from bottom to top.

- **Example: Applying Multiple Decorators**

```
def bold(func: Callable[..., str]) -> Callable[..., str]:
    def wrapper(*args: Any, **kwargs: Any) -> str:
        return f"<b>{func(*args, **kwargs)}</b>"

    return wrapper

def italic(func: Callable[..., str]) -> Callable[..., str]:
    def wrapper(*args: Any, **kwargs: Any) -> str:
        return f"<i>{func(*args, **kwargs)}</i>"

    return wrapper
```

```python
@bold
@italic
def greet(name: str) -> str:
    return f"Hello, {name}!"

print(greet("World"))  # Output: <b><i>Hello, World!</i></b>
```

- In this example, the @bold and @italic decorators are applied to the greet function. The @italic decorator is applied first, then the @bold decorator.

## 4. Advanced Techniques and Patterns

- **Decorator Factories that Take Arguments and Return Decorators:**

```python
from typing import Callable, TypeVar, ParamSpec, Any
import time

P = ParamSpec('P')
R = TypeVar('R')

def log_with_level(level: str) -> Callable[[Callable[P, Any]], Callable[P, Any]]:
    """
    A decorator factory that takes a logging level as an argument.
    """
    def decorator_function(func: Callable[P, Any]) -> Callable[P, Any]:
```

```python
    def wrapper_function(*args: P.args, **kwargs: P.kwargs)
-> Any:
        print(f"[{level}] Calling {func.__name__} with args:
{args}, kwargs: {kwargs}")
        result = func(*args, **kwargs)
        print(f"[{level}] {func.__name__} returned: {result}")
        return result
    return wrapper_function
  return decorator_function


@log_with_level("DEBUG")
def my_function(x: int, y: str) -> int:
  """My function does a thing."""
  return x * 2


my_function(3, "hello")
```

- The key here is the extra layer of nesting.
  log_with_level is a factory that produces a decorator.
- **Using Decorators to Implement Design Patterns:**
  Decorators can be used to implement design patterns
  like Singleton, Factory, or Observer in a more concise
  and elegant way.
- **Modifying Class Behavior with Decorators:**
  Class decorators can be used to add or modify class
  attributes, methods, or even change the class hierarchy.
  This can be useful for implementing mixins, adding
  functionality to existing classes, or enforcing coding
  standards.

## 5. Practical Applications

- **API Rate Limiting:** Decorators can limit the number of requests a client can make to an API within a certain time frame.

- **Automatic Retries:** Decorators can automatically retry failed operations, such as network requests or database queries.

- **Data Validation and Serialization:** Decorators can validate input data or automatically serialize/deserialize data when calling or returning from a function.

- **Dynamic Routing:** In web frameworks, decorators can be used to dynamically map URLs to handler functions.

- **AOP (Aspect-Oriented Programming):** Decorators can be used to implement aspects such as logging, security, or transaction management in a non-invasive way.

# CHAPTER 5

# *The Magic of Metaclasses: Controlling Class Creation*

---

*Understanding the Class Creation Process in Python*

In Python, classes are not just static blueprints; they are created dynamically through a well-defined process. Understanding this process is fundamental to grasping more advanced metaprogramming techniques like metaclasses and dynamic class generation.

## 1. The Default Class Creation Mechanism

- The type Metaclass: By default, all classes in Python are instances of the type metaclass. Metaclasses are responsible for creating classes.
- The class Statement: When you define a class using the class statement:

```python
class MyClass:
    """My custom class."""
    class_attribute = 10

    def __init__(self, x, y):
        self.x = x
```

```
    self.y = y

def my_method(self, z):
    return self.x + self.y + z
```

- Python internally performs a series of steps to create the MyClass object.
- **Steps Involved in Class Creation:**
  1. **Execution of Class Body:** The code within the class block is executed. This code typically consists of statements that define attributes (variables) and methods (functions) of the class.
  2. **Creation of Class Dictionary:** A dictionary is created to hold all the attributes and methods defined in the class body. This dictionary maps the names of the attributes and methods (e.g., 'class_attribute', '__init__', 'my_method') to their corresponding values.
  3. **Determining the Metaclass:** The metaclass to be used for creating the class is determined. If the class definition includes a metaclass argument, that metaclass is used. Otherwise, the metaclass of the base class(es) is used. If no base classes are specified, or if the base class is object, then the default metaclass, type, is used.
  4. **Class Creation:** The metaclass's __new__ method is called. This method is responsible for creating the class object in memory. It receives the class name, the tuple of base classes, and the dictionary of attributes as arguments.

5. **Class Initialization:** The metaclass's \_\_init\_\_ method is called. This method initializes the newly created class object.

## 2. The Role of the type Function

- **Creating Classes Dynamically:** The type function can also be used directly to create classes dynamically. Its alternate syntax is:

type(name, bases, dict)
  - name: The name of the class to create.
  - bases: A tuple of base classes.
  - dict: A dictionary containing the class's attributes and methods.
- Equivalence to class Statement: A class definition using the class statement is essentially syntactic sugar for calling type().
  - Example:

```
MyClass = type('MyClass', (object,), {
  'x': 10,
  'my_method': lambda self, z: self.x + z
})

obj = MyClass(5)
print(obj.x)
print(obj.my_method(20))
```

  - This is equivalent to:

```
class MyClass:
  x = 10

  def my_method(self, z):
    return self.x + z

obj = MyClass(5)
print(obj.x)
print(obj.my_method(20))
```

- **Relationship to Metaclasses:** When you call type() with the three-argument form, you are essentially calling the __call__ method of the default metaclass (type).

## 3. Customizing Class Creation with Metaclasses

- **Metaclasses:** Metaclasses are the classes of classes. They control how classes are created. By default, type is the metaclass for most classes.
- **Custom Metaclasses:** You can create custom metaclasses by inheriting from type and overriding its __new__ or __init__ methods. This allows you to hook into the class creation process and modify it.
- The __new__ Method: The __new__ method is responsible for creating the class object. It is called before __init__.
- The __init__ Method: The __init__ method is responsible for initializing the class object.
- Example:

```python
class MyMeta(type):
    def __new__(cls, name, bases, dct):
        print(f"Creating class {name}")
        # Modify the class dictionary before creating the class
        if 'extra_attribute' not in dct:
            dct['extra_attribute'] = 'Added by metaclass'
        return super().__new__(cls, name, bases, dct)

    def __init__(cls, name, bases, dct):
        super().__init__(name, bases, dct)
        print(f"Initializing class {name}")

class MyClass(metaclass=MyMeta):
    class_attribute = 10

    def my_method(self):
        pass

print(MyClass.extra_attribute)
```

- In this example, MyMeta is a custom metaclass. Its __new__ method adds an extra_attribute to the class, and its __init__ method prints a message during class initialization.

## 4. Dynamic Class Generation

- Metaclasses enable dynamic class generation, where you can create classes programmatically at runtime. This allows for highly flexible and adaptable code.

- Example

```
def create_class_dynamically(class_name, attributes):
    return type(class_name, (object,), attributes)

# Create a class with a dynamic name and attributes
MyDynamicClass                                           =
create_class_dynamically("RuntimeClass", {
    "dynamic_attribute": 42,
    "dynamic_method": lambda self: f"Hello from dynamic
method! attribute value: {self.dynamic_attribute}"
})

# Create an instance of the dynamically generated class
instance = MyDynamicClass()
print(instance.dynamic_attribute)  # Output: 42
print(instance.dynamic_method())
```

## 5. Benefits of Understanding the Class Creation Process

- **Metaprogramming:** A solid understanding of the class creation process is essential for effective metaprogramming, allowing you to create custom metaclasses and manipulate classes in advanced ways.
- **Framework Development:** Many Python frameworks rely on dynamic class creation and metaclasses to provide flexible and extensible architectures.
- **Code Generation:** You can leverage this knowledge to generate classes automatically based on data or configuration.

- **Customization:** Understanding the class creation process allows you to customize class behavior to meet specific requirements, such as enforcing coding standards or implementing design patterns.

*Introducing Metaclasses: Customizing Class Behavior at Creation Time*

Metaclasses are a powerful and often mysterious aspect of Python that provide a deep level of control over how classes are created. While most Python programmers may not need to use them regularly, understanding metaclasses is crucial for advanced metaprogramming and building highly adaptable and extensible systems.

## 1. The "Class of a Class"

To understand metaclasses, it's essential to remember that in Python, everything is an object, including classes themselves.

- **Instances and Classes:** An instance (or object) is created from a class. For example:

```
class MyClass:
    pass
```

```
obj = MyClass()  # obj is an instance of MyClass
```

- **Classes and Metaclasses:** A class, in turn, is an instance of a metaclass. By default, if you don't specify a metaclass, Python uses its built-in metaclass called type.

```
print(type(MyClass))  # Output: <class 'type'>
```

- This shows that MyClass is an instance of the type metaclass.
- **Analogy:**
    - A class is like a blueprint for creating objects (instances).
    - A metaclass is like a blueprint for creating classes.

## 2. The Default Metaclass: type

The built-in type is the default metaclass in Python. When you define a class using the class statement, Python uses type to create that class object.

```
class MyClass:
    pass

# This is what Python does, in simplified terms:
# MyClass = type('MyClass', (), {})
```

When you call MyClass(), you create an *instance* of MyClass. But when the Python interpreter executes the class MyClass statement, it calls type to create the MyClass *class*.

## 3. Custom Metaclasses

You can define your own metaclasses to customize the class creation process. To do this, you typically:

1. Create a class that inherits from type.
2. Override the __new__ or __init__ method (or both) to control class creation and initialization.
3. Specify your custom metaclass when defining a class using the metaclass keyword argument in the class definition.

```python
class MyMeta(type):
    def __new__(cls, name, bases, dct):
        """
        Called before __init__ to create the class object.
        """
        print(f"Creating class: {name}")
        # Modify the class dictionary (dct) before creating the class
        if 'extra_attribute' not in dct:
            dct['extra_attribute'] = 'Added by MyMeta'
        return super().__new__(cls, name, bases, dct)

    def __init__(cls, name, bases, dct):
        """
        Called after __new__ to initialize the class object.
        """
        super().__init__(name, bases, dct)
        print(f"Initializing class: {name}")

class MyClass(metaclass=MyMeta):
    class_attribute = 10
```

```
def my_method(self):
    pass
```

In this example:

- MyMeta is a custom metaclass that inherits from type.
- \_\_new\_\_ is overridden to add an extra_attribute to the class.
- \_\_init\_\_ is overridden to print a message during class initialization.
- metaclass=MyMeta in the MyClass definition tells Python to use MyMeta to create the MyClass class.

## 4. The Class Creation Process with a Metaclass

When a class is created with a custom metaclass:

1. The class body is executed, and a dictionary of attributes and methods is created.
2. The metaclass's \_\_new\_\_ method is called to create the class object.
3. The metaclass's \_\_init\_\_ method is called to initialize the class object.
4. The newly created class object is returned.

## 5. Why Use Metaclasses?

Metaclasses provide a powerful mechanism for controlling class creation, enabling you to:

- **Enforce Coding Standards:** Ensure that all classes adhere to certain conventions (e.g., requiring specific methods or attributes).
- **Automate Class Registration:** Automatically register classes with a central registry or framework.
- **Modify Class Behavior:** Dynamically add or modify methods or attributes.
- **Implement Design Patterns:** Enforce design patterns like Singleton or Abstract Base Class.
- **Create Domain-Specific Languages (DSLs):** Define the structure and behavior of classes in a DSL.
- **Code Generation:** Generate classes automatically based on external data.

## 6. Benefits for Adaptability and Extensibility

Metaclasses enhance adaptability and extensibility by allowing you to:

- **Dynamically Adapt Class Structures:** Modify class definitions at runtime based on changing requirements or external data.
- **Create Flexible Frameworks:** Build frameworks that can be easily extended by users who define their own classes.
- **Automate Boilerplate Code:** Reduce code duplication by automating the creation of repetitive class structures.

*Creating Custom Metaclasses to Enforce Standards and Add Functionality*

Metaclasses provide a powerful mechanism for controlling the class creation process in Python. By creating custom metaclasses, you can enforce specific standards, add functionality to classes automatically, and ensure consistency across your codebase. This leads to more robust, extensible, and maintainable applications.

## 1. Defining Custom Metaclasses

To create a custom metaclass, you typically follow these steps:

1. Inherit from type: Your custom metaclass should inherit from the built-in type metaclass. This provides the default behavior for class creation, which you can then customize.
2. Override __new__ or __init__ (or both):
   - __new__(cls, name, bases, dct): This special method is called *before* __init__ when a class is created. It's responsible for creating and returning the new class object.
     - cls: The metaclass itself.
     - name: The name of the class being created.
     - bases: A tuple of the base classes.
     - dct: A dictionary containing the class's attributes and methods.
   - __init__(cls, name, bases, dct): This method is called *after* __new__ to initialize the newly created class object.
     - cls: The class object that was just created.
     - name: The name of the class.
     - bases: A tuple of the base classes.

- **dct**: A dictionary containing the class's attributes and methods.

3. You typically override __new__ if you need to control the *creation* of the class object (e.g., modifying the class dictionary, changing the base classes). You override __init__ if you need to control the *initialization* of the class object after it has been created.

4. Use the metaclass keyword: When defining a class, you specify your custom metaclass using the metaclass keyword argument in the class definition.

## 2. Enforcing Standards

Custom metaclasses can be used to enforce coding standards and conventions within a project.

- **Example: Enforcing Attribute Naming Conventions**
  Suppose you want all class attributes in your project to be uppercase:

```python
class EnforceUppercaseAttrs(type):
    def __new__(cls, name, bases, dct):
        new_dct = {}
        for key, value in dct.items():
            if not key.startswith('__'): # Skip special methods
                if not key.isupper():
                    raise TypeError(f"Attribute '{key}' in class '{name}' must be uppercase")
            new_dct[key] = value
        return super().__new__(cls, name, bases, new_dct)
```

```python
class MyClass(metaclass=EnforceUppercaseAttrs):
    MY_ATTRIBUTE = 10  # Valid attribute name
    ANOTHER_ATTRIBUTE = "Hello"  # Valid attribute name
    __init__ = lambda self: None
    #my_attribute = 20  # Invalid attribute name (would raise
TypeError)

class BadClass(metaclass=EnforceUppercaseAttrs):
    bad_attribute = 20 # this will raise a TypeError
```

- In this example, the EnforceUppercaseAttrs metaclass ensures that all non-special attribute names in classes created with it are uppercase.
- Example: Ensuring Required Methods
  This metaclass ensures that any class has a specific method.

```python
class EnsureInterface(type):
    def __new__(cls, name, bases, dct):
        if "process" not in dct:
            raise TypeError(f"Class {name} must implement the
'process' method.")
        return super().__new__(cls, name, bases, dct)

class MyProcessor(metaclass=EnsureInterface):
    def __init__(self):
        print("created processor")
    def process(self, data):
        print(f"Processing data: {data}")
```

```python
class IncompleteProcessor(metaclass=EnsureInterface):
    def __init__(self):
        print("incomplete processor")
    pass  # Missing the required 'process' method;  TypeError
will be raised
```

## 3. Adding Functionality

Metaclasses can also be used to automatically add functionality to classes during their creation.

- **Example: Automatically Registering Classes**
  Suppose you're building a plugin system where you want to automatically register available plugins:

```python
class PluginRegistry(type):
    plugins = {}

    def __new__(cls, name, bases, dct):
        plugin_class = super().__new__(cls, name, bases, dct)
        if 'plugin_type' in dct:  # Only register classes with
'plugin_type'
            PluginRegistry.plugins[dct['plugin_type']] =
plugin_class
        return plugin_class

class BasePlugin(metaclass=PluginRegistry):
    pass  # All plugins should inherit from this

class ImageProcessor(BasePlugin):
    plugin_type = "image"
```

```python
    def process_image(self, image_data):
        print(f"Processing image data: {image_data}")

class TextProcessor(BasePlugin):
    plugin_type = "text"

    def process_text(self, text_data):
        print(f"Processing text data: {text_data}")

print(PluginRegistry.plugins)
# Output: {'image': <class '__main__.ImageProcessor'>, 'text':
<class '__main__.TextProcessor'>}
```

- In this example, the PluginRegistry metaclass automatically registers any class that inherits from BasePlugin and has a plugin_type attribute. This eliminates the need for manual registration.
- Example: Adding a Common Method
  This metaclass adds a method to every class.

```python
class AddLoggerMeta(type):
    def __new__(cls, name, bases, dct):
        def log(self, message):
            print(f"[{name}] {message}")
        dct['log'] = log
        return super().__new__(cls, name, bases, dct)

class MyClass(metaclass=AddLoggerMeta):
    def do_something(self):
        self.log("Doing something")  # Now has the log method
```

```
obj = MyClass()
obj.do_something()
```

## 4. Benefits

- **Consistency**: Metaclasses enforce standards, leading to more consistent code.
- **Automation**: They automate tasks like registration, reducing boilerplate.
- **Extensibility**: They make it easier to extend frameworks and libraries.
- **Dynamic Adaptation**: They enable dynamic modification of class behavior.

*Use Cases for Metaclasses: Abstract Base Classes, Singletons, and More*

Metaclasses, while often considered an advanced topic, can be incredibly useful for solving specific design problems and creating more robust and flexible code. Here are some common use cases:

### 1. Abstract Base Classes (ABCs)

- **Problem:**
  - You want to define a common interface for a set of classes, ensuring that they all implement certain methods.
  - You want to prevent users from instantiating a base class that is meant to be a template for its subclasses.
- **Solution:**

o While Python has the abc module for defining abstract base classes, metaclasses can also be used to achieve similar results, sometimes with more flexibility.

- **Example:**

```python
import abc


class MyMeta(type):
    def __new__(cls, name, bases, dct):
        if '__init__' in dct and '__call__' not in dct:
            raise TypeError(f"Class {name} must implement __call__ method")
        return super().__new__(cls, name, bases, dct)


class BaseProcessor(metaclass=MyMeta):  #can't be instantiated without implementing __call__
    def __init__(self, config):
        self.config = config


class ImageProcessor(BaseProcessor): # no error, because it implements __call__
    def __init__(self, config):
        super().__init__(config)
    def __call__(self, data):
        print(f"Processing image: {data}")


class TextProcessor(BaseProcessor): # error, because it doesn't implement __call__
    def __init__(self, config):
        super().__init__(config)
```

Pass

- In this example, the MyMeta metaclass ensures that any class inheriting from BaseProcessor implements the __call__ method.
- **Benefits**:
    - Enforces interface compliance at class definition time, preventing runtime errors.
    - Provides a more explicit way to define and enforce interfaces compared to relying solely on documentation or convention.

## 2. Singletons

- **Problem:**
    - You want to ensure that only one instance of a class can exist.
- **Solution:**
    - Metaclasses can be used to control the instantiation process and ensure that only a single instance is ever created.
- **Example:**

```python
class Singleton(type):
    _instances = {}

    def __call__(cls, *args, **kwargs):
        if cls not in cls._instances:
            cls._instances[cls] = super().__call__(*args, **kwargs)
        return cls._instances[cls]
```

```
class GlobalSettings(metaclass=Singleton):
   def __init__(self, config_file):
      self.config_file = config_file
      # Load settings from config_file

settings1 = GlobalSettings("config.ini")
settings2 = GlobalSettings("config.ini")   # Returns the same
instance as settings1

print(settings1 is settings2) # Output: True
```

- In this example, the Singleton metaclass ensures that only one instance of the GlobalSettings class is ever created, no matter how many times you try to instantiate it.
- **Benefits**:
    - Guarantees a single point of access to a resource, preventing potential conflicts or inconsistencies.
    - Provides a clean and elegant way to implement the Singleton pattern.

## 3. Dynamically Creating Classes

- **Problem:**
    - You need to create classes with different attributes or methods based on external data, configuration, or runtime conditions.
- **Solution**:
    - Metaclasses can be used to generate classes dynamically, tailoring them to specific needs.

- **Example**:

```
class ClassFactory(type):
    def __new__(cls, name, bases, dct, fields):
        """
        Creates a class with attributes defined by 'fields'.
        """
        new_dct = {}
        for field_name, field_type in fields.items():
            def getter(self, name=field_name):
                return getattr(self, "_" + name)

            def setter(self, value, name=field_name):
                if not isinstance(value, field_type):
                    raise TypeError(f"'{name}' must be of type {field_type.__name__}")
                setattr(self, "_" + name, value)

            new_dct[field_name] = property(getter, setter)
        return super().__new__(cls, name, bases, {**dct, **new_dct})


def create_data_class(name, fields):
    return ClassFactory(name, (object,), {}, fields=fields)


# Dynamically create a class for representing a user
User = create_data_class("User", {"name": str, "age": int, "email": str})


user1 = User(name="John Doe", age=30, email="john.doe@example.com")
```

```
print(user1.name, user1.age, user1.email)

user1.age = 31
print(user1.age)

#user1.age = "thirty"  # Raises TypeError
```

- Here, the ClassFactory metaclass takes a dictionary of fields (name and type) and dynamically creates a class with corresponding properties.
- **Benefits**:
    - Reduces code duplication when creating many similar classes.
    - Allows you to define class structures based on external data.
    - Enables the creation of highly adaptable and flexible systems.

## *LET'S DELVE DEEPER INTO CLASS DECORATORS WITH MORE ELABORATE EXAMPLES TO ILLUSTRATE THEIR VERSATILITY.*

### 1. Modifying Class Attributes and Methods

- **Example 1: Adding a Class-Level Registry**
  Imagine you're building a system where you want to keep track of all registered classes of a certain type. A class decorator can automate this registration process:

```
from typing import Dict, Type
```

```python
class Registry:
    """A class decorator to register classes."""

    registry: Dict[str, Type] = {}  # Class-level registry

    def __init__(self, cls: type):
        """Initializes the decorator with the class to be decorated."""
        self.cls = cls
        Registry.registry[cls.__name__] = cls  # Register the class

    def __call__(self, *args: Any, **kwargs: Any) -> object:
        """
        Creates an instance of the decorated class.
        """
        return self.cls(*args, **kwargs)  # Create and return an instance of the class

@Registry
class Component:
    """A base class for components."""

    def __init__(self, name: str):
        self.name: str = name

@Registry
class Button(Component):
    """A button component."""
```

```python
    def __init__(self, name: str, label: str):
        super().__init__(name)
        self.label: str = label

    def render(self) -> str:
        return f"<button>{self.label}</button>"

@Registry
class InputField(Component):
    """An input field component."""

    def __init__(self, name: str, placeholder: str):
        super().__init__(name)
        self.placeholder: str = placeholder

    def render(self) -> str:
        return f"<input type='text' placeholder='{self.placeholder}'>"

# The registry now contains the component classes
print(Registry.registry)
# You can access the classes from the registry to create
instances
button = Registry.registry["Button"]("my_button",
"Click me")
print(button.render())
```

In this example, the Registry class decorator automatically registers any class decorated with it into a class-level registry.

This allows you to easily access and manage different types of components in your application.

- **Example 2: Modifying Class Methods**
  Here's how you can use a class decorator to modify the methods of a class:

```python
from typing import Callable, TypeVar, ParamSpec, Any


P = ParamSpec('P')
R = TypeVar('R')


def add_logging(cls: type) -> type:
    """A class decorator to add logging to all methods of a class."""
    for name, method in cls.__dict__.items():
        if callable(method) and not name.startswith("__"):
# Decorate only methods
            original_method: Callable[P, R] = method  # type: ignore


            def logged_method(self: Any, *args: P.args, **kwargs: P.kwargs) -> R:
                """Wrapper to add logging."""
                print(f"Calling method: {cls.__name__}.{name} with args: {args}, kwargs: {kwargs}")
                result: R = original_method(self, *args, **kwargs)
```

```python
            print(f"Method {cls.__name__}.{name}
returned: {result}")
            return result

        setattr(cls, name, logged_method) # Replace the
original method with the wrapped version
    return cls


@add_logging
class MyClass:
    def __init__(self, x: int, y: int) -> None:
        self.x: int = x
        self.y: int = y

    def add(self, z: int) -> int:
        return self.x + self.y + z

    def multiply(self, a: int, b: int) -> int:
        return self.x * a + self.y * b

obj = MyClass(1, 2)
obj.add(3)
obj.multiply(4, 5)
```

- The add_logging decorator adds logging to the add and multiply methods of MyClass without modifying the original methods directly.

## 2. Enhancing Class Functionality

- **Example 1: Adding a Class Factory Method**

```python
from typing import Type, TypeVar, Any, Dict

T = TypeVar('T', bound='Base')

def factory(cls: Type[T]) -> Type[T]:
    """Adds a 'create' class method to create instances
from dictionaries."""
    @classmethod
    def create(cls, data: Dict[str, Any]) -> T:
        """Creates an instance of the class from a
dictionary."""
        instance = cls(**data)
        return instance

    cls.create = create
    return cls

@factory
class User:
    def __init__(self, name: str, age: int, email: str):
        self.name: str = name
        self.age: int = age
        self.email: str = email

user_data = {"name": "Jane Doe", "age": 28, "email":
"jane.doe@example.com"}
user = User.create(user_data)  # Use the new 'create'
class method
print(user.name, user.age, user.email)
```

- The @factory decorator adds a create class method to the User class, allowing instances to be created directly from dictionaries.
- **Example 2: Implementing an Interface**

```python
import abc


class MyInterface(abc.ABC):
    @abc.abstractmethod
    def process(self, data: str) -> str:
        raise NotImplementedError


def implements_interface(interface_class: type[MyInterface]):
    """A class decorator to ensure a class implements a given interface."""
    def decorator(cls: type) -> type:
        if not issubclass(cls, interface_class):
            raise TypeError(f"Class {cls.__name__} must implement interface {interface_class.__name__}")
        return cls
    return decorator


class MyProcessor:

    def process(self, data: str) -> str:


        return f"Processed: {data}"


@implements_interface(MyInterface)
```

175

```
#  @implements_interface(MyInterface)    # If this
decorator is applied, a TypeError will be raised


# class BadProcessor:


#    pass
```

- The implements_interface decorator ensures that the decorated class implements a specific interface (defined as an ABC).

These examples demonstrate the flexibility and power of class decorators in Python. They allow you to dynamically modify and enhance classes, promoting code reuse, consistency, and adaptability.

### Advanced Metaclass Techniques and Best PracticeS

Metaclasses, while powerful, can also introduce complexity if not used carefully. Here, we delve into advanced techniques and best practices for using them effectively.

### 1. Metaclass Composition

- **Problem:** When dealing with multiple inheritance, you might face conflicts if the parent classes have different metaclasses.
- **Solution:** Metaclass composition involves creating a new metaclass that inherits from the metaclasses of the parent classes. This allows you to combine the behavior of multiple metaclasses.

- **Example:**

```python
class Meta1(type):
    def __new__(cls, name, bases, dct):
        print(f"Meta1 creating {name}")
        return super().__new__(cls, name, bases, dct)

class Meta2(type):
    def __new__(cls, name, bases, dct):
        print(f"Meta2 creating {name}")
        return super().__new__(cls, name, bases, dct)

class MyClass(metaclass=Meta1): #inherits from object
    Pass

class MyClass2(metaclass=Meta2):   #inherits   from object
    pass

class CombinedClass(MyClass, MyClass2):   #inherits from MyClass and MyClass2
    pass

print(type(CombinedClass))
```

- In this case, the metaclass of CombinedClass is type, which is the default. To combine the functionality of Meta1 and Meta2, you would need to create a new metaclass that inherits from both. This is complex and not always recommended, and in most cases multiple inheritance can be avoided.

## 2. Metaclasses and Class Decorators

- **Problem:** You want to apply some modifications to a class, but the modification logic might be complex and better suited to a separate function or class.
- **Solution:** You can combine metaclasses and class decorators to achieve a more modular and organized approach.
- **Example:**

```python
def add_default_attribute(cls):
    if not hasattr(cls, "default_value"):
        cls.default_value = 100
    return cls


class MyMeta(type):
    def __new__(cls, name, bases, dct):
        decorated_class = super().__new__(cls, name, bases, dct)
        return add_default_attribute(decorated_class)  # Apply the decorator here


class MyClass(metaclass=MyMeta):
    pass


print(MyClass.default_value)  # Output: 100
```

- Here, the class decorator @add_default_attribute is applied during the class creation process, which is managed by the MyMeta metaclass. This pattern allows you to separate the class modification logic into a reusable decorator.

# 3. Using __prepare__

- **Problem:** You need to control the namespace in which the class body is executed.
- **Solution:** The __prepare__ method of a metaclass allows you to specify the dictionary that will be used as the class's namespace before the class body is executed.
- **Example:**

```python
from collections import OrderedDict

class OrderedClassNamespace(type):
    @classmethod
    def __prepare__(metacls, name, bases):
        return OrderedDict()  # Use an ordered dictionary

    def __new__(cls, name, bases, dct):
        cls_obj = super().__new__(cls, name, bases, dct)
        cls_obj._ordered_keys = list(dct.keys())
        return cls_obj

class MyClass(metaclass=OrderedClassNamespace):
    z = 3
    y = 2
    x = 1

print(MyClass._ordered_keys)  # Output: ['__module__',
'__qualname__', 'z', 'y', 'x']
```

- In this example, the order of attributes is preserved using the OrderedClassNamespace metaclass.

## 4. Best Practices

- **Use Metaclasses Sparingly:** Metaclasses add complexity to your code. Use them only when they provide a clear advantage over simpler solutions like class decorators or factory functions.
- **Keep Metaclasses Simple:** Avoid putting too much logic into your metaclasses. Complex metaclasses can be difficult to understand and debug.
- **Follow Naming Conventions:**
  - Use a naming convention (e.g., adding "Meta" to the class name) to clearly identify metaclasses.
- **Document Metaclasses Thoroughly:** Explain the purpose and behavior of your metaclasses with clear and concise documentation.
- **Test Metaclasses Carefully:** Thoroughly test any code that uses metaclasses to ensure it behaves as expected.
- **Consider Alternatives:** Before using a metaclass, consider if other techniques, such as class decorators, class factories, or mixins, can achieve the same result with less complexity.

# CHAPTER 6

## Fine-Grained Control with Attribute Access and Descriptors

---

*Controlling Attribute Access in Python*

Python provides special methods that allow you to intercept and customize how attributes are accessed, set, or deleted on objects. These methods are crucial for creating objects with dynamic behavior and adaptable logic.

### 1. The Default Attribute Access Mechanism

When you access an attribute of an object (e.g., obj.my_attr), Python follows a specific process:

1. Check the instance's __dict__: Python first looks for the attribute in the object's instance dictionary (obj.__dict__). This dictionary stores the object's instance attributes.
2. Check the class's __dict__: If the attribute is not found in the instance dictionary, Python looks in the class's dictionary (obj.__class__.__dict__). This dictionary stores class attributes, methods, and other class-level definitions.

3. **Check the base classes:** If the attribute is not found in the class dictionary, Python checks the dictionaries of the class's base classes, following the Method Resolution Order (MRO).
4. Call __getattr__ (if defined): If the attribute is not found in any of the above locations, and the class defines a __getattr__ method, that method is called to provide a fallback mechanism.
5. Raise AttributeError: If the attribute is not found and __getattr__ is not defined, Python raises an AttributeError.

When you set or delete an attribute (obj.my_attr = value, del obj.my_attr), Python directly modifies the object's __dict__ by default.


## 2. Customizing Attribute Access with Special Methods

To customize this default behavior, you can define special methods in your classes:

- __getattr__(self, name):
    - Called when an attribute lookup fails to find the attribute in the usual places (i.e., in the instance's __dict__ and the class's MRO).
    - The name parameter is a string containing the name of the attribute being accessed.
    - This method should either return the value of the attribute or raise an AttributeError.
    - This allows you to provide dynamic attribute access, such as calculating an attribute's value on

demand or handling requests for missing attributes.

- __setattr__(self, name, value):
  - Called when an attribute assignment is attempted on an instance (e.g., obj.my_attr = value).
  - The name parameter is a string containing the name of the attribute being set, and value is the value being assigned to it.
  - This method allows you to customize how attribute values are set, such as performing validation, logging changes, or updating related attributes.
  - Inside __setattr__, to avoid infinite recursion, you should use super().__setattr__(name, value) (or object.__setattr__(self, name, value)) to assign the attribute.
- __delattr__(self, name):
  - Called when an attribute deletion is attempted on an instance (e.g., del obj.my_attr).
  - The name parameter is a string containing the name of the attribute being deleted.
  - This method allows you to customize how attributes are deleted, such as preventing deletion of certain attributes or performing cleanup actions.

## 3. Examples

- Example 1: Dynamic Attribute Generation with __getattr__

```python
class DynamicAttributes:
    def __init__(self):
        self._data = {}  # Store attributes in a dictionary

    def __getattr__(self, name):
        if name in self._data:
            return self._data[name]
        else:
            # Calculate the attribute value if it's not in _data
            if name.startswith("computed_"):
                value = len(name)  # Example computation
                self._data[name] = value  # Store the computed value
                return value
            raise AttributeError(f"DynamicAttributes' object has no attribute '{name}'")

    def __setattr__(self, name, value):
        if name != "_data":  # Prevent direct modification of _data
            self._data[name] = value
        else:
            super().__setattr__(name, value)


obj = DynamicAttributes()
obj.abc = 123  # Sets attribute 'abc'
print(obj.abc)  # Output: 123
print(obj.computed_xyz)      #    Output:    12    (computed dynamically)
print(obj.computed_pqr)  # Output: 12
```

In this example, __getattr__ is used to dynamically generate attributes whose names start with "computed_".

- Example 2: Attribute Validation with __setattr__

```
class Person:
    def __init__(self, name, age):
        self.name = name
        self.age = age

    def __setattr__(self, name, value):
        if name == "age":
            if not isinstance(value, int):
                raise TypeError("Age must be an integer")
            if value < 0 or value > 120:
                raise ValueError("Age must be between 0 and 120")
        super().__setattr__(name, value)  # Call the default behavior


person = Person("Alice", 30)
person.age = 35  # OK
# person.age = "invalid"  # Raises TypeError
# person.age = 150  # Raises ValueError
person.name = "Bob" # OK
print(person.name, person.age)
```

Here, __setattr__ is used to validate the value being assigned to the 'age' attribute.

- Example 3: Preventing Attribute Deletion with __delattr__

```
class Config:
    def __init__(self, setting1, setting2):
        self.setting1 = setting1
        self.setting2 = setting2
        self._read_only = ("setting1")  # Attributes that cannot be deleted

    def __delattr__(self, name):
        if name in self._read_only:
            raise AttributeError(f"Cannot delete read-only attribute '{name}'")
        else:
            super().__delattr__(name)

config = Config("value1", "value2")
# del config.setting1   # Raises AttributeError: Cannot delete read-only attribute 'setting1'
del config.setting2  # OK
print(config.setting2)
```

- In this case, __delattr__ prevents the deletion of the 'setting1' attribute, while allowing the deletion of other attributes.

## 4. Relevance to Adaptability and Extensibility

- **Dynamic Attribute Management:** These special methods enable you to create objects whose attributes can be dynamically accessed, modified, or even created at runtime. This is essential for building systems that can adapt to changing data structures or external requirements.

- **Customizable Object Behavior:** By defining these methods, you can tailor how objects respond to attribute access, allowing for more flexible and extensible object models.

- **Creating Proxies:** __getattr__ can be used to create proxy objects that delegate attribute access to another object, enabling you to add functionality or modify behavior without changing the original object.

- **Implementing Descriptors:** These methods are related to the descriptor protocol, which provides a powerful way to manage attribute access for properties, methods, and other object attributes. Descriptors are explained in the next section of the book.

## *The Descriptor Protocol in Python*

The descriptor protocol is a powerful feature in Python that allows you to customize how attributes are accessed, set, and deleted. Descriptors provide a way to implement managed attributes, offering greater control than simple instance variables.

## 1. What is a Descriptor?

A descriptor is an object that implements one or more of the following methods:

- __get__(self, instance, owner): Called when the attribute is accessed (e.g., obj.my_descriptor).

- __set__(self, instance, value): Called when the attribute is set (e.g., obj.my_descriptor = value).
- __delete__(self, instance): Called when the attribute is deleted (e.g., del obj.my_descriptor).

Where:

- self: The descriptor instance itself.
- instance: The instance of the class where the attribute is accessed, set, or deleted. If the descriptor is accessed through the class (e.g., MyClass.my_descriptor), instance is None.
- owner: The class of the instance.

## 2. Types of Descriptors

- Data Descriptors: Implement both __get__ and __set__ (and optionally __delete__). They control attribute access and setting.
- Non-Data Descriptors: Implement only __get__. They are primarily used for implementing read-only attributes or computed properties.

## 3. How Descriptors Work

When an attribute is accessed, set, or deleted on an object, Python's attribute access mechanism checks if the attribute is a descriptor. If it is, the corresponding descriptor method (__get__, __set__, or __delete__) is invoked.

4. Examples

- Example 1: A Simple Data Descriptor

```python
class Validated:
    def __init__(self, attribute_name):
        self.attribute_name = attribute_name
        self._storage_name = f"_{attribute_name}"  # Store the actual value with a different name

    def __get__(self, instance, owner):
        print(f"Getting {self.attribute_name}")
        if instance is None:
            return self
        return getattr(instance, self._storage_name)

    def __set__(self, instance, value):
        print(f"Setting {self.attribute_name} to {value}")
        if not isinstance(value, int):
            raise TypeError(f"{self.attribute_name} must be an integer")
        setattr(instance, self._storage_name, value)

    def __delete__(self, instance):
        print(f"Deleting {self.attribute_name}")
        delattr(instance, self._storage_name)

class MyClass:
    my_attr = Validated("my_attr")  # Create a descriptor instance

    def __init__(self, initial_value):
```

```
    self.my_attr = initial_value  # Use the descriptor to set the
initial value

obj = MyClass(10)
print(obj.my_attr)  # Access the attribute (calls __get__)
obj.my_attr = 20  # Set the attribute (calls __set__)
del obj.my_attr  # Delete the attribute (calls __delete__)
```

In this example, Validated is a data descriptor that enforces type validation for the my_attr attribute.

- Example 2: A Non-Data Descriptor for a Read-Only Property

```
import math

class Circle:
    def __init__(self, radius):
        self.radius = radius

    class Area:  # Non-data descriptor
        def __get__(self, instance, owner):
            if instance is None:
                return self
            return math.pi * instance.radius**2

    area = Area()  # Create a descriptor instance

circle = Circle(5)
print(circle.area)  # Access the 'area' property (calls __get__)
```

# circle.area = 10  # Raises AttributeError: can't set attribute (because it's a non-data descriptor)

Here, Area is a non-data descriptor that computes the area of a circle. It's read-only because it only implements __get__.

## 5. Descriptors and Properties

Properties are a convenient way to define managed attributes, and they are implemented using descriptors.

- property(fget=None, fset=None, fdel=None, doc=None): The built-in property() function creates a descriptor.
- Example:

```python
class MyClass:
    def __init__(self, _x):
        self.x = _x

    def get_x(self):
        return self.x

    def set_x(self, value):
        if value < 0:
            raise ValueError("x must be non-negative")
        self.x = value

    x = property(get_x, set_x, None, "The x property")

obj = MyClass(10)
print(obj.x)  # Calls get_x
obj.x = 20  # Calls set_x
```

```
# obj.x = -5  # Raises ValueError
print(MyClass.__dict__['x'].__class__)
```

## 6. Relevance to Adaptability and Extensibility

- **Managed Attributes:** Descriptors allow you to manage attribute access, enabling you to add behavior like validation, lazy loading, and computed properties.
- **Dynamic Behavior:** They make objects more dynamic by allowing attribute behavior to be customized at runtime.
- **Code Reusability:** Descriptors can be reused across multiple classes to enforce consistent attribute management.
- **Framework Development:** Descriptors are often used in frameworks and libraries to provide a clean and flexible way for users to define and use attributes.

## *Creating Custom Descriptors in Python for Efficient Attribute Management*

Descriptors are a powerful feature in Python that allows you to control how attributes are accessed, set, and deleted. By creating custom descriptors, you can implement managed attributes with additional behavior, such as data validation, type checking, and lazy loading, leading to more efficient, robust, and adaptable code.

## 1. Understanding Descriptors

A descriptor is an object that implements one or more of the descriptor protocol methods:

- __get__(self, instance, owner): Called when the attribute is accessed.
- __set__(self, instance, value): Called when the attribute is set.
- __delete__(self, instance): Called when the attribute is deleted.

Where:

- self: The descriptor instance itself.
- instance: The instance of the class where the attribute is accessed, set, or deleted. If the descriptor is accessed through the class (e.g., MyClass.my_descriptor), instance is None.
- owner: The class of the instance.

## 2. Data Validation and Type Checking

Descriptors are ideal for enforcing data validation and type constraints on attributes.

- **Example: Validating Attribute Type and Range**

```
class ValidatedNumber:

    def __init__(self, name, expected_type, min_value=None,
max_value=None):

        self.name = name

        self.expected_type = expected_type

        self.min_value = min_value
        self.max_value = max_value
```

```python
        self._storage_name = f"_{name}"  # Store the actual
value with a private name

    def __get__(self, instance, owner):
        if instance is None:
            return self
        return getattr(instance, self._storage_name)

    def __set__(self, instance, value):
        if not isinstance(value, self.expected_type):
            raise TypeError(f"{self.name} must be a
{self.expected_type.__name__}")
        if self.min_value is not None and value < self.min_value:
            raise ValueError(f"{self.name} must be >=
{self.min_value}")
        if self.max_value is not None and value > self.max_value:
            raise ValueError(f"{self.name} must be <=
{self.max_value}")
        setattr(instance, self._storage_name, value)

    def __delete__(self, instance):
        delattr(instance, self._storage_name)

class Circle:
    radius = ValidatedNumber("radius", int, min_value=0)

    def __init__(self, radius):
        self.radius = radius

    def area(self):
```

```
      return 3.14159 * self.radius**2

c = Circle(10)  # Works
c.radius = 20  # Works
# c.radius = -5  # Raises ValueError
# c.radius = "abc"  # Raises TypeError
print(c.area())
```

In this example, ValidatedNumber ensures that the radius attribute of the Circle class is an integer and falls within a specified range.

### 3. Lazy Loading

Descriptors can also be used to implement lazy loading, where an attribute's value is only computed when it's first accessed. This can improve performance by deferring expensive computations.

- **Example: Lazy Loading a Database Connection**

```
import sqlite3

class DatabaseConnection:
    def __init__(self, db_name):
        self.db_name = db_name

    class Connection:
        def __get__(self, instance, owner):
            if instance is None:
                return self
```

```python
        if not hasattr(instance, '_connection'):
                print(f"Connecting to database:
{instance.db_name}")
                instance._connection =
sqlite3.connect(instance.db_name) # Establish connection
        return instance._connection

    def __set__(self, instance, value):
        raise AttributeError("Cannot set connection. It is a
lazy-loaded property")

    def __delete__(self, instance):
        if hasattr(instance, '_connection'):
                print(f"Closing database connection:
{instance.db_name}")
            instance._connection.close()
            del instance._connection

    connection = Connection()


db = DatabaseConnection("mydatabase.db")
# Connection is not established until it is accessed.

conn1 = db.connection    # Establishes and returns the
connection
conn2 = db.connection  # Returns the existing connection

print(conn1 is conn2) # True, same connection object

del db.connection
```

In this example, the Connection descriptor establishes a database connection only when the db.connection attribute is first accessed. Subsequent accesses return the same connection object.

## 4. Computed Properties

* Descriptors are helpful when you want to create attributes that are computed dynamically.

- **Example: A computed property for a class**

```
class Rectangle:
    def __init__(self, length, width):
        self._length = length
        self._width = width

    class Area:
        def __get__(self, instance, owner):
            if instance is None:
                return self
            return instance._length * instance._width

    area = Area()

    def __set__(self, instance, value):
        raise AttributeError("Cannot set area. It is a computed property")

    def __delete__(self, instance):
        print("Deleting the area")
```

```
    del instance._length
    del instance._width

rectangle = Rectangle(4, 5)
print(rectangle.area)  # Output: 20
# rectangle.area = 10   # Raises AttributeError: can't set
attribute

del rectangle.area # deletes length and width
```

## 5. Benefits

- **Data Integrity**: Descriptors enforce data validation and type checking, preventing invalid data from being assigned to attributes.
- **Efficiency**: Lazy loading defers expensive computations until they are actually needed, improving performance.
- **Code Reusability**: Descriptors can be reused across multiple classes to manage attributes consistently.
- **Abstraction**: They provide a clean way to encapsulate attribute management logic, making your code more organized and maintainable.
- **Flexibility**: Descriptors offer a high degree of customization, allowing you to tailor attribute behavior to specific needs.

*HERE ARE MORE EXAMPLES & CODE SNIPPETS TO SOLIDIFY YOUR UNDERSTANDING OF PRACTICAL APPLICATIONS OF DESCRIPTORS IN PYTHON*

Descriptors are a powerful tool for managing attribute access in Python, enabling you to build robust and efficient classes. Here are some practical applications that demonstrate their real-world benefits:

## 1. Data Validation and Type Checking

- **Problem:** You need to ensure that attributes of your class adhere to specific data types and constraints.
- **Solution:** Use descriptors to enforce validation rules when attributes are set.
- **Example:**

```python
class ValidatedString:

    def __init__(self, name, min_length=0, max_length=None):

        self.name = name

        self.min_length = min_length

        self.max_length = max_length

        self._storage_name = f"_{name}"

    def __get__(self, instance, owner):

        if instance is None:
            return self
        return getattr(instance, self._storage_name)

    def __set__(self, instance, value):
        if not isinstance(value, str):
            raise TypeError(f"{self.name} must be a string")
        if len(value) < self.min_length:
```

```python
                raise ValueError(f"{self.name} must be >=
{self.min_length} characters")
            if self.max_length is not None and len(value) >
self.max_length:
                raise ValueError(f"{self.name} must be <=
{self.max_length} characters")
        setattr(instance, self._storage_name, value)

    def __delete__(self, instance):
        delattr(instance, self._storage_name)

class User:
    username = ValidatedString("username", min_length=5,
max_length=20)
    email = ValidatedString("email", min_length=6,
max_length=50)

    def __init__(self, username, email):

        self.username = username

        self.email = email

user = User("johndoe", "john.doe@example.com")  # Works

user.username = "jane_doe"  # Works

# user.username = "short"  # Raises ValueError

# user.email = 123  # Raises TypeError
```

In this example, ValidatedString ensures that the username and email attributes of the User class are strings that meet the specified length requirements.

## 2. Lazy Loading

- **Problem:** You have attributes whose values are expensive to compute or retrieve (e.g., accessing a database, making a network request). You want to defer these computations until the attribute is actually accessed.
- **Solution:** Use descriptors to implement lazy loading.
- **Example: Lazy Loading with Caching**

```python
import urllib.request
import json


class URLContent:
    def __init__(self, url):
        self.url = url

    class Content:
        def __get__(self, instance, owner):
            if instance is None:
                return self
            if not hasattr(instance, '_content'):
                print(f"Fetching content from {instance.url}")
                try:
                    with urllib.request.urlopen(instance.url) as response:
                        data = response.read().decode('utf-8')
```

```python
            instance._content = json.loads(data)  # Parse the
content as JSON
        except Exception as e:
            raise AttributeError(f"Could not retrieve or parse
content from {instance.url}: {e}")
        return instance._content

    content = Content()

# Example Usage
url1                                                          =
URLContent("https://jsonplaceholder.typicode.com/todos/1")
# The content is not fetched until it is accessed

data1 = url1.content  # Fetches and caches the content
print(data1)
data2 = url1.content  # Returns the cached content
print(data2)
```

- In this example, the Content descriptor fetches the content from the URL only when it's first accessed. Subsequent accesses return the cached content, avoiding redundant network requests.

### 3. Computed Properties

- **Problem:** You want to create attributes that are calculated dynamically based on other attributes, but you don't want to recalculate them every time they are accessed.

- **Solution:** Use a non-data descriptor (__get__ only) to define a computed property.
- **Example: A computed property for a class**

```python
class Circle:
    def __init__(self, radius):
        self.radius = radius

    class Area:  # Non-data descriptor
        def __get__(self, instance, owner):
            if instance is None:
                return self
            return 3.14159 * instance.radius**2

    area = Area()  # Create a descriptor instance

    @property
    def diameter(self):
        return self.radius * 2

circle = Circle(5)
print(circle.area)
print(circle.diameter)
```

- In this example, the area is calculated dynamically

## 4. Attribute Validation with Multiple Constraints

- **Problem:** You need to apply multiple validation rules to an attribute, such as type checking, range checks, and format validation.

- **Solution:** Create a descriptor that encapsulates all the validation logic.

```python
import re


class ValidatedString:
    def __init__(self, name, validations=None):
        self.name = name
        self.validations = validations or []
        self._storage_name = f"_{name}"

    def __get__(self, instance, owner):
        if instance is None:
            return self
        return getattr(instance, self._storage_name)

    def __set__(self, instance, value):
        if not isinstance(value, str):
            raise TypeError(f"{self.name} must be a string")
        for validation in self.validations:
            if not validation(value):
                raise ValueError(f"{self.name} failed validation: {validation.__name__}")
        setattr(instance, self._storage_name, value)

    def __delete__(self, instance):
        delattr(instance, self._storage_name)


def min_length(n):
```

```python
    def validator(value):
        return len(value) >= n
        validator.__name__ = f"min_length_{n}"    # Set a
meaningful name for the validation function
    return validator

def max_length(n):
    def validator(value):
        return len(value) <= n
    validator.__name__ = f"max_length_{n}"
    return validator

def email_format(value):
    return re.match(r"[^@]+@[^@]+\.[^@]+", value) is not
None
email_format.__name__ = "email_format"

class User:
                    email    =    ValidatedString("email",
validations=[min_length(6), max_length(50), email_format])

    def __init__(self, email):

        self.email = email

user = User("valid.email@test.com")  # Works

# user.email = "invalid"  # Raises ValueError (min_length)

# user.email = "too_long_email_address@test.com"  # Raises
ValueError (max_length)
```

```
# user.email = "not_an_email"    # Raises ValueError
(email_format)
```

This example uses a list of validation functions to enforce multiple constraints on the 'email' attribute.

These examples demonstrate how descriptors can be used to create robust and efficient classes by:

- Enforcing data integrity through validation and type checking
- Optimizing performance with lazy loading
- Providing a clean and reusable way to manage attribute behavior

*Understanding the Relationship Between Descriptors and Properties in Python*

Descriptors and properties are both mechanisms in Python for managing attribute access, but they serve slightly different purposes and are implemented differently. Understanding their relationship is crucial for effective object-oriented programming.

**1. Descriptors**

- **Definition:** A descriptor is an object that implements one or more of the descriptor protocol methods:
  - __get__(self, instance, owner): Called when the attribute is accessed.

- o \_\_set\_\_(self, instance, value): Called when the attribute is set.
  - o \_\_delete\_\_(self, instance): Called when the attribute is deleted.
- **Purpose:** Descriptors provide a low-level mechanism for controlling attribute access. They allow you to define custom behavior for how attributes are retrieved, set, and deleted.
- **Usage:** You create a descriptor by defining a class with \_\_get\_\_, \_\_set\_\_, or \_\_delete\_\_ methods. Then, you make an instance of this descriptor class a class attribute of another class.
- **Example:**

```python
class MyDescriptor:
    def __get__(self, instance, owner):
        if instance is None:
            return self
        return instance._my_attr_value  # Access the stored value

    def __set__(self, instance, value):
        if value < 0:
            raise ValueError("Value must be non-negative")
        instance._my_attr_value = value  # Store the value

class MyClass:
    my_attr = MyDescriptor("my_attr")  # Descriptor instance is
a class attribute

    def __init__(self, initial_value):
```

```
    self.my_attr = initial_value

obj = MyClass(10)
print(obj.my_attr)  # Accesses using __get__
obj.my_attr = 20  # Sets using __set__
# obj.my_attr = -5  # Raises ValueError
```

## 2. Properties

- **Definition:** Properties provide a more Pythonic and convenient way to define managed attributes. They allow you to access an instance attribute like a regular attribute, but with added functionality.
- **Purpose:** Properties are typically used to:
  - Encapsulate attribute access: Control how an attribute is read and written.
  - Implement computed attributes: Calculate an attribute's value dynamically.
  - Provide a cleaner interface: Accessing a property looks like accessing a regular attribute, even though there's underlying logic.
- **Usage:** You define a property using the built-in property() function or the @property decorator.
- **Example:**

```
class MyClass:
  def __init__(self, _x):
    self._x = _x


  @property
  def x(self):
    """Getter for the 'x' property."""
```

```python
        return self._x

    @x.setter
    def x(self, value):
        """Setter for the 'x' property."""
        if value < 0:
            raise ValueError("x must be non-negative")
        self._x = value

    @x.deleter
    def x(self):
        """Deleter for the 'x' property."""
        del self._x

obj = MyClass(10)
print(obj.x)  # Access like a regular attribute
obj.x = 20  # Set like a regular attribute
del obj.x
```

## 3. Relationship

- **Properties are built on descriptors:** A property is actually a type of descriptor. When you define a property, Python creates a descriptor object internally.
- property() creates descriptors: The property() built-in is a shortcut for creating descriptors without defining a separate class. It bundles the getter, setter, and deleter functions into a single property object.
- **Descriptors are more general:** Descriptors are a more general mechanism. You can create custom descriptor

classes to implement various attribute management patterns beyond what properties directly provide.

## 4. Key Differences and When to Use Which

| Feature | Descriptors | Properties |
|---------|-------------|------------|
| Implementation | Define a class with __get__, __set__, __delete__ | Use the property() built-in or @property decorator |
| Complexity | More verbose, lower-level | More concise, higher-level |
| Flexibility | Highly flexible; can implement complex attribute management logic | Designed specifically for managing a single attribute |
| Common Use Cases | Implementing data validation, lazy loading, | Creating managed attributes with getters, setters, and deleters |

| | advanced attribute access patterns | |
|---|---|---|
| | | |

**When to Use:**

- Use **properties** for simple managed attributes where you need to control access to a single attribute in a straightforward way (e.g., for encapsulation or adding validation to a specific attribute).
- Use **descriptors** when you need more general and reusable solutions for managing attributes, such as:
  - Implementing complex validation logic that needs to be applied to multiple attributes.
  - Creating attributes that compute their values in a sophisticated way (e.g., lazy loading, computed properties with dependencies).
  - Defining custom attribute access patterns that go beyond simple getting, setting, and deleting.

# CHAPTER 7

# *Transforming Code with Abstract Syntax Trees (AST)*

*Introduction to Abstract Syntax Trees (ASTs) and Code Representation*

In programming, an Abstract Syntax Tree (AST) is a tree representation of the abstract syntactic structure of source code written in a programming language. It represents the structure of the code in a way that is independent of the details of the specific syntax. ASTs are crucial for enabling powerful dynamic code analysis and modification.

## 1. What is an Abstract Syntax Tree (AST)?

- **Syntax Tree:** A syntax tree is a tree representation of the syntactic structure of source code. Each node in the tree represents a construct in the code, such as an expression, statement, or declaration.
- **Abstract:** The term "abstract" emphasizes that the AST focuses on the essential syntactic structure, omitting details like:
    - Parentheses and braces
    - Commas and semicolons
    - Specific keywords

- **Code Representation:** ASTs provide a structured and hierarchical representation of code, making it easier for programs to understand and manipulate the code's logic.

## 2. How Code is Represented

Source code, which is human-readable text, needs to be transformed into a format that a computer can process efficiently. This transformation typically involves several stages:

1. **Lexing (Lexical Analysis):** The source code is broken down into a stream of tokens, which are the basic building blocks of the language (e.g., keywords, identifiers, operators, literals).
2. **Parsing:** The tokens are then organized into a syntax tree according to the grammar of the programming language. This syntax tree represents the syntactic structure of the code.
3. **Abstract Syntax Tree (AST) Generation:** The syntax tree is further processed to remove non-essential details, resulting in an AST. The AST retains the essential structure but is more abstract and easier to work with.

## 3. The ast Module in Python

Python provides the ast module in its standard library, which allows you to:

- **Parse Python code into an AST:** The ast.parse() function takes a source code string as input and returns an AST object.
- **Traverse the AST:** You can walk through the nodes of the AST using functions like ast.walk().
- **Manipulate the AST:** You can modify the AST by adding, removing, or changing nodes.
- **Generate code from an AST:** The ast module can be used in conjunction with other libraries like astor to generate Python code from a modified AST.

## 4. Key Components of an AST

An AST consists of nodes, where each node represents a specific language construct. Common node types in a Python AST include:

- **Module:** The root node, representing the entire code.
- **FunctionDef:** A function definition.
- **ClassDef:** A class definition.
- **Assign:** An assignment statement.
- **Expr:** An expression statement.
- **Call:** A function call.
- **Name:** A variable name.
- **Num:** A numeric literal.
- **Str:** A string literal.
- **BinOp:** A binary operator (e.g., +, -, *, /).
- **If:** An if statement.
- **For:** A for loop.

Each node has attributes that provide information about the corresponding code construct. For example, a FunctionDef node has attributes like name (the function name), args (the arguments), and body (the function body).

## 5. Example: Parsing Code into an AST

```
import ast

code_string = "def greet(name):\n        print(f'Hello,
{name}!')\ngreet('World')"
ast_tree = ast.parse(code_string)
print(ast.dump(ast_tree, indent=4))
```

In this example, the ast.parse() function converts the Python code string into an AST. The ast.dump() function then provides a string representation of the AST.

## 6. Benefits of Using ASTs

- **Structured Representation:** ASTs provide a structured and hierarchical representation of code, making it easier to analyze and manipulate compared to raw text.
- **Language Independence:** ASTs abstract away syntactic variations, allowing you to work with the code's logic regardless of formatting or minor syntactic differences.
- **Code Analysis:** ASTs enable powerful code analysis techniques, such as:
  - Static analysis: Detecting potential errors or code quality issues without executing the code.

- Code understanding: Analyzing code structure and dependencies.
- **Code Modification:** ASTs make it possible to modify code programmatically, allowing you to:
  - Automate code refactoring.
  - Generate code dynamically.
  - Transform code for optimization or other purposes.
- **Metaprogramming:** ASTs are a fundamental tool for metaprogramming, enabling you to write code that manipulates other code.

*Exploring the ast Module for Analyzing Python Code Programmatically*

The ast module in Python provides a way to work with the Abstract Syntax Tree (AST) of Python code. ASTs are a tree representation of the syntactic structure of the code, making it easier to analyze and manipulate programmatically. This capability is crucial for building efficient code analysis tools and performing metaprogramming.

**1. Abstract Syntax Trees (ASTs)**

- **What is an AST?**
  - An AST is a hierarchical representation of the structure of source code.
  - Each node in the tree represents a construct in the code, such as a function definition, a class definition, a statement, or an expression.

- ASTs omit syntactic details that are not essential to the code's meaning, such as parentheses, commas, and whitespace.
- **Benefits of ASTs:**
  - **Structured Representation:** ASTs provide a clear and organized way to represent code, making it easier to traverse and analyze programmatically.
  - **Abstraction:** ASTs abstract away from the specific syntax of the language, allowing you to focus on the code's underlying logic.
  - **Code Manipulation:** ASTs can be modified, allowing you to transform code programmatically.

## 2. The ast Module

Python's ast module provides classes and functions to work with ASTs.

- **Parsing Code:**
  - The ast.parse(source, filename, mode) function parses Python source code into an AST object.
    - source: The source code string.
    - filename: The name of the file being parsed (can be a dummy value if parsing a string).
    - mode: The mode in which the code should be parsed:
      - 'exec': For a module or a sequence of statements.
      - 'eval': For a single expression.

- **'single'**: For a single interactive statement.
- **AST Node Objects:**
  - The ast module defines a set of classes that represent different types of AST nodes. Each node has attributes that store information about the corresponding code construct.
  - For example:
    - ast.FunctionDef: Represents a function definition.
      - Attributes: name (function name), args (arguments), body (statements in the function body).
    - ast.Assign: Represents an assignment statement.
      - Attributes: targets (list of targets to assign to), value (the value being assigned).
    - ast.Call: Represents a function call.
      - Attributes: func (the function being called), args (arguments passed to the function).
    - ast.If: Represents an if statement
      - Attributes: test (the condition), body (statements in the if block), orelse (statements in the else block).
- **Traversing the AST:**
  - The ast.walk(node) function recursively traverses the AST, yielding each node in the tree.
- **Dumping the AST:**

o The ast.dump(node, indent=None) function returns a formatted string representation of the AST, which is helpful for debugging and understanding the tree structure.

## 3. Example: Parsing and Traversing an AST

```python
import ast

code_string = """
def greet(name):
    if name:
        print(f"Hello, {name}!")
    else:
        print("Hello, World!")
greet("User")
"""

ast_tree = ast.parse(code_string)  # Parse the code into an AST

def visit_node(node):
    """A simple visitor function to print information about each node."""
    print(f"Node Type: {type(node).__name__}")
    if isinstance(node, ast.FunctionDef):
        print(f" Function Name: {node.name}")
        for arg in node.args.args:
            print(f" Argument: {arg.arg}")
    elif isinstance(node, ast.Call):
```

```
                              print(f"       Function      Call:
{node.func.value.id}.{node.func.attr}")

for node in ast.walk(ast_tree):  # Traverse the AST
  visit_node(node)
```

This example parses a simple Python function and then traverses the AST, printing information about each node encountered.

### 4. Applications of ASTs

Analyzing ASTs enables various powerful applications:

- **Static Analysis:**
    - ASTs allow you to analyze code without executing it.
    - This can be used to detect potential errors, enforce coding standards, identify security vulnerabilities, and optimize code.
    - Tools like linters (e.g., Pylint, Flake8) and static type checkers (e.g., MyPy) often use ASTs.
- **Code Refactoring:**
    - ASTs make it possible to modify code structure programmatically, which is essential for automating refactoring tasks.
    - For example, you can write a tool that uses ASTs to automatically rename variables, extract code into functions, or change the order of statements.
- **Code Generation:**

- ASTs can be used to generate Python code dynamically.
- This is useful for tasks such as creating code from templates, generating boilerplate code, or building domain-specific languages (DSLs).
- **Metaprogramming:**
  - ASTs are a fundamental tool for metaprogramming, where programs manipulate other programs.
  - They allow you to write code that can analyze, transform, and generate Python code.

*Traversing and Manipulating ASTs in Python*

Abstract Syntax Trees (ASTs) provide a structured representation of code, and the ast module in Python allows you to work with them programmatically. Being able to traverse and manipulate ASTs enables powerful techniques for code analysis, modification, and generation.

**1. Traversing the AST**

Traversing an AST involves visiting each node in the tree to examine its contents. The ast module provides the ast.walk() function for this purpose.

- ast.walk(node):
  - Recursively traverses the AST, yielding each node in the tree.
  - The nodes are visited in no particular order.
- **Example: Traversing an AST and Printing Node Types**

```python
import ast

code_string = """
def my_function(x, y):
    z = x + y
    return z * 2

result = my_function(3, 4)
print(result)
"""

ast_tree = ast.parse(code_string)

for node in ast.walk(ast_tree):
    print(type(node).__name__)
```

- This code will print the type of each node in the AST, such as FunctionDef, arguments, Assign, BinOp, Return, and Call.

## 2. Manipulating the AST

The real power of ASTs comes from your ability to modify them. You can change the structure of the code represented by the AST by adding, removing, or modifying its nodes.

- **Example 1: Changing a Variable Name**

```python
import ast
import astor  # You might need to install this: pip install astor
```

```python
code_string = "x = 10\nprint(x)"
ast_tree = ast.parse(code_string)

for node in ast.walk(ast_tree):
    if isinstance(node, ast.Name) and node.id == 'x':
        node.id = 'y'  # Change variable name from 'x' to 'y'

modified_code = astor.to_source(ast_tree)   # Generate code from the modified AST
print(modified_code)  # Output: y = 10\nprint(y)

exec(modified_code)  # Execute the modified code
```

In this example, the code changes every occurrence of the variable x to y.

- **Example 2: Adding a Function Call**

```python
import ast
import astor

code_string = "def my_function():\n    pass"

ast_tree = ast.parse(code_string)

# Create an ast.Call node to represent print("Hello")
print_call = ast.Call(
    func=ast.Name(id='print', ctx=ast.Load()),  # Call the 'print' function
    args=[ast.Str(s='Hello')],   # Pass the string 'Hello' as an argument
```

```python
    keywords=[],
    starargs=None,
    kwargs=None
)

# Create an ast.Expr node to wrap the ast.Call
print_expr = ast.Expr(value=print_call)

# Add the print call to the function body
for node in ast.walk(ast_tree):
    if isinstance(node, ast.FunctionDef) and node.name ==
'my_function':
        node.body.append(print_expr)  # Append the print call to
the function's body
        break

modified_code = astor.to_source(ast_tree)
print(modified_code)

exec(modified_code)
```

This example adds a print("Hello") call to the end of the my_function function.

## 3. Applications

- **Automated Code Refactoring:** You can write tools that use ASTs to automate complex refactoring tasks, such as renaming variables, extracting code into functions, or restructuring code blocks.

- **Code Generation:** ASTs can be used to generate code dynamically, which is useful for creating code from templates or generating boilerplate code.
- **Static Analysis:** ASTs enable advanced static analysis techniques, allowing you to detect potential errors, enforce coding standards, or identify security vulnerabilities in code without executing it.
- **Compiler Optimization:** Compilers use ASTs to optimize code before generating machine code.
- **Metaprogramming:** ASTs are a fundamental tool for metaprogramming, where programs manipulate other programs.

## *Use Cases for AST Manipulation in Python*

Abstract Syntax Trees (ASTs) provide a powerful way to represent code structure, and manipulating them allows for various applications in code analysis, modification, and generation. Here are some key use cases:

## 1. Code Linting

- **Problem:** You want to enforce coding standards and identify potential style issues or errors in your code.
- **Solution:** ASTs can be used to analyze the code structure and check for compliance with specific rules.
- **Example:**

```python
import ast

code_string = """
```

```python
def my_function(arg1, Arg2):  # Non-compliant variable name
    if arg1 > 10:
        a = 10 # Non-compliant variable name
        return a + Arg2
    else:
        return arg1
"""

ast_tree = ast.parse(code_string)

def check_naming_convention(node):
    """Checks if variable names follow a convention (e.g.,
lowercase)."""
    if isinstance(node, ast.Name) and not node.id.islower():
        print(f"Violation: Variable name '{node.id}' should be
lowercase (Line {node.lineno})")

for node in ast.walk(ast_tree):
    check_naming_convention(node)
```

- A linter like flake8 uses ASTs to check code style.
- **Benefits:**
    - Improves code quality and consistency.
    - Catches errors early in the development process.
    - Enforces coding standards across a project.

## 2. Code Refactoring

- **Problem:** You want to automate the process of restructuring code to improve its readability, maintainability, or performance.
- **Solution:** ASTs can be used to modify the code structure programmatically, enabling automated refactoring.
- **Example: Automated Variable Renaming**

```python
import ast
import astor

code_string = """
def calculate_sum(x, y):
    s = x + y
    return s

result = calculate_sum(10, 20)
print(result)
"""

ast_tree = ast.parse(code_string)

def rename_variable(node, old_name, new_name):
    """Renames a variable in the AST."""
    if isinstance(node, ast.Name) and node.id == old_name:
        node.id = new_name

for node in ast.walk(ast_tree):
    rename_variable(node, 's', 'total_sum')  # Rename variable 's'
to 'total_sum'

modified_code = astor.to_source(ast_tree)
```

```
print(modified_code)

exec(modified_code)
```

- Tools like Rope or Jedi use ASTs for refactoring.
- **Benefits:**
    - Automates tedious and error-prone refactoring tasks.
    - Ensures that code transformations are applied consistently.
    - Reduces the risk of introducing bugs during refactoring.

## 3. Static Analysis

- **Problem:** You want to analyze code for potential issues or properties without executing it.
- **Solution:** ASTs enable static analysis, where you can examine the code's structure to infer information about its behavior.
- **Example: Detecting Unused Variables**

```python
import ast

code_string = """
def my_function():
    a = 10
    b = 20
    c = a + b
    print(c)
    return a
```

```python
"""

ast_tree = ast.parse(code_string)

def find_unused_variables(node):
    """Finds variables that are assigned but not used."""
    assigned_vars = set()
    used_vars = set()

    for child in ast.walk(node):
        if isinstance(child, ast.Name):
            if isinstance(child.ctx, ast.Store):
                assigned_vars.add(child.id)
            elif isinstance(child.ctx, ast.Load):
                used_vars.add(child.id)

    unused_vars = assigned_vars - used_vars
    for var in unused_vars:
        print(f"Unused variable: {var}")

for node in ast.walk(ast_tree):
    if isinstance(node, ast.FunctionDef):
        find_unused_variables(node) # Analyze variables within functions
```

- Tools like Pyflakes use ASTs for static analysis.
- **Benefits:**
    - Detects potential errors before runtime.
    - Provides insights into code behavior without execution.

- Enables automated code review and analysis.

## *Building Custom Code Transformation Tools with the ast Module*

The ast module in Python allows you to work with Abstract Syntax Trees (ASTs), which are tree-like representations of the syntactic structure of your code. By traversing and manipulating ASTs, you can create powerful tools that modify code programmatically. This capability is essential for advanced metaprogramming and building adaptable systems.

### 1. Core Concepts

- **Abstract Syntax Trees (ASTs):**
    - A hierarchical representation of code structure.
    - Nodes represent code constructs (e.g., functions, classes, statements).
    - The ast module provides classes to represent these nodes.
- **AST Traversal:**
    - The ast.walk(node) function allows you to traverse the AST and visit each node.
- **AST Manipulation:**
    - You can modify the AST by changing node attributes, adding new nodes, or removing existing ones.
- **Code Generation:**
    - Libraries like astor can be used to generate Python code from a modified AST.

## 2. Building a Code Transformation Tool

Here's a general approach to building a custom code transformation tool using the ast module:

1. **Parse the Code:**
   - Use ast.parse(source_code) to convert the source code into an AST.
2. **Traverse the AST:**
   - Use ast.walk(ast_tree) to visit each node in the AST.
3. **Identify Nodes to Modify:**
   - Use conditional statements (e.g., isinstance()) to check the type of each node and identify the code constructs you want to change.
4. **Modify the AST:**
   - Modify the attributes of the nodes you want to change, or add/remove nodes as needed.
5. **Generate the Modified Code:**
   - Use astor.to_source(ast_tree) to generate Python code from the modified AST.

## 3. Example: Adding Logging to Function Calls

Let's create a tool that automatically adds logging statements to the beginning and end of every function call in a given code snippet:

```
import ast
import astor
import inspect
import sys
```

```python
def add_logging_to_function_calls(code_string):
    """
    Adds logging statements before and after each function call
    in the given code.
    """

    ast_tree = ast.parse(code_string)  # Parse the code into an AST


    def add_logging_to_call(node):
        """Adds logging calls before and after a function call."""
        if isinstance(node, ast.Call):
            # Create logging statements
            log_before = ast.Expr(
                value=ast.Call(
                    func=ast.Name(id='print', ctx=ast.Load()),
                    args=[ast.Str(s=f"Calling {astor.to_source(node.func)} with args: {node.args}")],
                    keywords=[],
                    starargs=None,
                    kwargs=None,
                )
            )

            log_after = ast.Expr(
                value=ast.Call(
                    func=ast.Name(id='print', ctx=ast.Load()),
                    args=[ast.Str(s=f"{astor.to_source(node.func)} returned: {{result}}")],
                    keywords=[],
```

```
        starargs=None,
        kwargs=None,
    )
)

    # Create a temporary variable to store the result of the
function call
        result_var = ast.Name(id='_result', ctx=ast.Store())
            assign_result = ast.Assign(targets=[result_var],
value=node)

    #insert the logging statements

    nonlocal_vars = set()
    for n in ast.walk(node):
            if isinstance(n, ast.Name) and isinstance(n.ctx,
ast.Store):
            nonlocal_vars.add(n.id)

    if len(nonlocal_vars) > 0:

        wrapper_body = [
        log_before,
        assign_result, # Store the result
        log_after,
        ast.Return(value = result_var)
        ]
    else:
        wrapper_body = [
        log_before,
```

```python
            node, # Call the original function
        log_after,
    ]

    new_func = ast.FunctionDef(
                    name=f"wrapped_{node.func.attr if
isinstance(node.func, ast.Attribute) else node.func.id}",    #
Generate a unique name
        args=node.func.args,
        body=wrapper_body,
        decorator_list=[], # Remove any decorators from the
call
        returns=None
    )

    return new_func
    return node

class Transformer(ast.NodeTransformer):
    def visit_Call(self, node):
        return add_logging_to_call(node) #wrap the function
call

transformer = Transformer()
modified_ast = transformer.visit(ast_tree)

modified_code = astor.to_source(modified_ast)
print("Modified Code:")
print(modified_code)
```

```
exec(modified_code)

# Example usage:
# original_code = """
# def my_function(x, y):
#     return x + y
#
# result = my_function(3, 4)
# print(result)
# """
#
#              modified_code          =
add_logging_to_function_calls(original_code)
# print(modified_code)
# exec(modified_code)


```

In this example, the `add_logging_to_function_calls` function uses the `ast.NodeTransformer` to find function calls and insert logging statements before and after them.

## 4. Key Techniques
* **`ast.NodeTransformer`:**
   * A subclass of `ast.NodeVisitor` that allows you to modify nodes in the AST.
   * You override the `visit_NodeType()` methods to define how to transform specific node types.
   * The `generic_visit()` method traverses the children of a node.

* **`ast.NodeVisitor`:**
    * A class that facilitates traversing an AST.
        * You subclass it and override the `visit_NodeType()` methods to define actions to be performed when visiting nodes of a particular type.
* **Creating New Nodes:**
    * You can create new AST nodes using the `ast` module's node classes (e.g., `ast.Call`, `ast.Name`, `ast.Expr`).
* **Generating Code:**
    * The `astor` library can be used to generate source code from a modified AST.

## 5. Applications

* **Code Optimization:** You can create tools to analyze an AST and apply optimizations, such as removing redundant code or simplifying expressions.
* **Automatic Documentation Generation:** You can extract information from ASTs to generate API documentation.
* **Code Obfuscation/Deobfuscation:** You can transform ASTs to make code harder or easier to understand, respectively.
* **Static Analysis Tools**: Tools like Pylint use ASTs.

# CHAPTER 8

# Building Extensible Applications with Metaprogramming

---

*Designing for Extensibility: The Central Role of Metaprogramming*

Extensibility is a crucial aspect of software design, referring to the ability to add new features or modify existing ones without altering the core structure of the system. Metaprogramming, with its capacity to manipulate code at runtime, plays a central role in achieving this goal. Let's explore how.

## 1. The Challenge of Extensibility

Traditional software development often involves writing code that is static and fixed at the time of development. This can make it challenging to accommodate new requirements or changing circumstances without modifying the core codebase, which can introduce bugs, break compatibility, and increase maintenance costs.

## 2. Metaprogramming to the Rescue

Metaprogramming provides techniques to overcome these challenges by enabling you to write code that can:

- **Inspect** its own structure and behavior.
- **Modify** existing code.
- **Generate** new code dynamically.

This allows you to design systems that are inherently more flexible and adaptable to change.

### 3. How Metaprogramming Enables Extensibility

Here are several ways in which metaprogramming facilitates the design of extensible applications:

- **Dynamic Class and Object Creation:**
  - Metaprogramming allows you to create new classes or objects at runtime, based on external data or runtime conditions.
  - This is useful for scenarios where the structure of the data or the required behavior is not known until the program is running.
  - For example, you can create classes to represent different data formats or adapt to new API endpoints without changing the core application code.
- **Decorators for Aspect-Oriented Programming:**
  - Decorators enable you to add functionality to functions or methods without modifying their core logic.
  - This is particularly useful for implementing cross-cutting concerns, such as logging, authentication, or caching, which apply to multiple parts of the application.

- By using decorators, you can keep your core code clean and focused on its primary task, while adding extensions in a modular way.
- **Metaclasses for Class Customization:**
  - Metaclasses provide fine-grained control over the class creation process.
  - You can use them to enforce coding standards, automatically register classes with a registry, or even generate entire class hierarchies dynamically.
  - This allows you to define a common behavior for a family of classes, ensuring consistency and simplifying extension.
- **Plugin Architectures:**
  - Metaprogramming is essential for building plugin architectures, where external modules can be loaded and integrated into the application at runtime.
  - This allows you to add new features or support new data formats without modifying the core application.

## 4. Benefits of Designing for Extensibility with Metaprogramming

- **Reduced Code Modification:** New features can be added with minimal or no changes to the existing codebase.

- **Increased Reusability:** Metaprogramming techniques promote the creation of reusable components and extension points.
- **Improved Maintainability:** Code becomes more modular and easier to maintain, as extensions are kept separate from the core logic.
- **Enhanced Flexibility:** Applications can adapt to changing requirements, new technologies, or diverse user needs.
- **Faster Development:** New features can be added more quickly, as developers can leverage existing extension points.

## 5. Examples of Metaprogramming for Extensibility

- **Example 1: Plugin System with Dynamic Loading**

```python
import importlib
import os

def load_plugins(plugin_dir):
    """Loads plugins from a specified directory."""
    plugins = {}
    for filename in os.listdir(plugin_dir):
        if filename.endswith(".py"):
            module_name = filename[:-3]
            try:
                module = importlib.import_module(f"{plugin_dir}.{module_name}")
                if hasattr(module, "register"):
```

```
            plugin_instance = module.register()  # Get plugin
instance
            plugins[module_name] = plugin_instance
            print(f"Loaded plugin: {module_name}")
      except Exception as e:
            print(f"Error loading plugin {module_name}: {e}")
    return plugins


# Assume a directory named "plugins" contains plugin
modules
plugins = load_plugins("plugins")


# Use the plugins
for plugin_name, plugin in plugins.items():
   # dynamically use the plugin
   # print(plugin.process())
   pass
```

- This example demonstrates how to dynamically load modules from a directory, effectively creating a plugin system.
- **Example 2: Configuration-Driven Class Creation**

```
import json

def create_class_from_config(config_file):
    """Creates a class dynamically from a JSON configuration
file."""
  with open(config_file, "r") as f:
    config = json.load(f)

  class_name = config.get("name", "DynamicClass")
```

```python
    attributes = config.get("attributes", {})

    def __init__(self, *args, **kwargs):
                    for i, (attr_name, attr_value) in
enumerate(attributes.items()):
        if i < len(args):
            setattr(self, attr_name, args[i])
        elif key in kwargs:
            setattr(self, attr_name, kwargs[key])
        else:
            setattr(self, attr_name, None) # or a default
    dynamic_class = type(class_name, (object,), {
        "__init__": __init__, # Use the dynamically created
__init__
    })
    return dynamic_class

# config.json
'''
{
  "name": "MyDataClass",
  "attributes": {
    "field1": "int",
    "field2": "str",
    "field3": "float"
  }
}
'''
```

```
MyDataClass = create_class_from_config("config.json")  #
Create a class from config

instance = MyDataClass(10, "hello", 3.14)
print(instance.field1, instance.field2, instance.field3)  #
Output: 10 hello 3.14
'''
config file
'''
```

- This example creates a class dynamically based on a configuration file, allowing you to define the class structure without writing code directly.

## Implementing Plugin Architectures with Dynamic Module Loading

A plugin architecture allows you to extend the functionality of an application without modifying its core code. Dynamic module loading is a key technique for achieving this in Python, enabling you to load and integrate external modules at runtime.

### 1. What is a Plugin Architecture?

In a plugin architecture:

- The main application defines a set of interfaces or extension points.
- Plugins are external modules that implement these interfaces.

- The application can discover and load plugins at runtime.
- New functionality can be added by installing new plugins, without changing the application's core code.

This approach promotes modularity, extensibility, and customization.

## 2. Dynamic Module Loading with importlib

Python's importlib module provides the necessary tools for dynamic module loading.

- importlib.import_module(name, package=None): This function imports a module by its name. The name argument is a string specifying the module to import.

## 3. Implementing a Plugin System

Here's a step-by-step guide to implementing a simple plugin system using dynamic module loading:

1. **Define a Plugin Interface:**
    - Create an abstract base class (ABC) or a simple protocol that defines the methods that a plugin must implement. This provides a standard interface for all plugins.

```
import abc

class PluginInterface(abc.ABC):
```

```
"""
Interface that all plugins must implement.
"""

@abc.abstractmethod
def process(self, data):
    """Processes the input data and returns the result."""
    raise NotImplementedError
```

2. **Create Plugin Modules:**
   - Create separate Python files (modules) for each plugin.
   - Each plugin module should:
     - Import the plugin interface.
     - Define a class that implements the interface.
     - Include a register() function that returns an instance of the plugin class.
   - Example plugin (plugins/my_plugin.py):

```
from plugin_interface import PluginInterface   # Import the interface

class MyPlugin(PluginInterface):
    """
    A sample plugin.
    """

    def __init__(self, config):
        """Initialize the plugin with configuration data."""
```

```python
        self.config = config
        print(f"MyPlugin initialized with config: {self.config}")

    def process(self, data):
        """Processes the data."""
        return f"MyPlugin processed data: {data}"

def register(config=None):
    """
    Returns an instance of the plugin class.
    """
    return MyPlugin(config)
```

3. **Discover and Load Plugins:**
   o The main application should:
     ▪ Specify a directory where plugins are located.
     ▪ Use os.listdir() or similar to get a list of files in the directory.
     ▪ Filter for Python files.
     ▪ Dynamically import each plugin module using importlib.import_module().
     ▪ Call the register() function in each module to get a plugin instance.
     ▪ Store the plugin instances in a dictionary or list for later use.

4. **Use the Plugins:**

- The main application can then use the loaded plugin instances to perform specific tasks, without needing to know their concrete classes in advance.

## 4. Example: A Simple Plugin System

```python
import importlib
import os
from typing import Dict, Any

# Define a simple plugin interface (in a separate file, e.g.,
plugin_interface.py)
class PluginInterface:
    """
    Base class for all plugins.
    """
    def process(self, data: str) -> str:
        raise NotImplementedError("Subclasses must implement the process method")

def load_plugins(plugin_dir: str, config: Dict[str, Any]) -> Dict[str, PluginInterface]:
    """
    Loads plugins from a specified directory.

    Args:
        plugin_dir: The directory where plugin modules are located.
        config: A dictionary of configuration data to pass to the plugins.
```

Returns:
    A dictionary of plugin instances, keyed by plugin name.
    """

```python
plugins: Dict[str, PluginInterface] = {}
for filename in os.listdir(plugin_dir):
            if filename.endswith(".py") and not filename.startswith("__"): # Filter for Python files
        module_name = filename[:-3]  # Remove ".py" extension
        module_path = f"{plugin_dir}.{module_name}"
        try:
            module = importlib.import_module(module_path) # Import the module
            if hasattr(module, "register"):
                plugin_instance = module.register(config)  # Get plugin instance
                plugins[module_name] = plugin_instance
                print(f"Loaded plugin: {module_name}")
            else:
                print(f"Plugin {module_name} does not have a register function")
        except Exception as e:
            print(f"Failed to load plugin {module_name}: {e}")
    return plugins
```

```python
if __name__ == "__main__":
    # Create a dummy plugin directory and plugin file
    if not os.path.exists("plugins"):
        os.makedirs("plugins")

    with open("plugins/my_plugin.py", "w") as f:
        f.write(
            """
from plugins.plugin_interface import PluginInterface

class MyPlugin(PluginInterface):
    def __init__(self, config):
        self.config = config
        print(f"MyPlugin loaded with config: {config}")

    def process(self, data):
        return f"MyPlugin processed: {data} with config {self.config}"

def register(config):
    return MyPlugin(config)
"""
        )

    # Load the plugins
    plugin_config = {"param1": "value1", "param2": "value2"}
    loaded_plugins = load_plugins("plugins", plugin_config)

    # Use the plugins
    for plugin_name, plugin in loaded_plugins.items():
```

```
data = "some_data"
result = plugin.process(data)
print(f"Plugin '{plugin_name}' returned: {result}")
```

## 5. Benefits of Plugin Architectures

- **Extensibility**: Add new features without modifying the core application.
- **Modularity**: Decompose the application into smaller, independent modules.
- **Customization**: Allow users to customize the application's behavior.
- **Maintainability**: Easier to maintain and update plugins separately.
- **Faster Development**: Develop new features as separate plugins.

### *Using Metaclasses and Decorators to Automate Extension Mechanisms*

Metaclasses and decorators are powerful tools in Python that can be combined to automate the process of creating extensible systems. They allow you to streamline how new functionality is added to your application, ensuring consistency, reducing boilerplate code, and promoting a more adaptable architecture.

## 1. The Challenge of Extensibility

When designing extensible systems, you often face the challenge of:

- **Registering Extensions:** New components (e.g., plugins, modules, classes) need to be registered with the system so they can be discovered and used.
- **Enforcing Interfaces:** Extensions should adhere to a specific interface or contract to ensure compatibility.
- **Configuration:** Extensions may require specific configuration or initialization steps.
- **Reducing Boilerplate:** The process of creating and integrating new extensions should be as simple and straightforward as possible for developers.

## 2. Metaclasses and Decorators to Automate Extension

Metaclasses and decorators can work in tandem to address these challenges and automate extension mechanisms.

### 2.1. Metaclasses for Automatic Registration and Enforcement

- **Metaclasses** can control the class creation process. This allows you to:
    - Automatically register new extension classes when they are defined.
    - Enforce that extension classes adhere to a specific interface or inherit from a particular base class.
    - Modify the class definition to add common attributes or methods.
- **Example: Automatic Plugin Registration**

```
import abc

class PluginRegistry(type):
```

```python
    """
    A metaclass that automatically registers plugins.
    """

    plugins: dict[str, type] = {}  # Class-level registry of plugins

    def __new__(cls, name, bases, dct):
        plugin_class = super().__new__(cls, name, bases, dct)  # Create the class
        if "plugin_type" in dct:
            PluginRegistry.plugins[dct["plugin_type"]] = plugin_class  # Register by plugin_type
        return plugin_class

class BasePlugin(metaclass=PluginRegistry):
    """
    Base class for all plugins.  All plugins must inherit from this.
    """

    def __init__(self, config):
        self.config = config

    @classmethod
    @abc.abstractmethod
    def get_plugin_type(cls) -> str:
        """Returns the type of plugin."""
        return cls.plugin_type

class ImageProcessor(BasePlugin):
```

```python
    """
    A plugin for processing images.
    """

    plugin_type = "image"  # Plugin type for registration

    def process(self, data):
        """Processes image data."""
        print(f"Processing image with config: {self.config}")
        return f"Processed image: {data}"

class TextProcessor(BasePlugin):
    """
    A plugin for processing text.
    """

    plugin_type = "text"  # Plugin type for registration

    def process(self, text):
        """Processes text data."""
        return f"Processed text: {text}"

# The plugins are automatically registered in
PluginRegistry.plugins

print(PluginRegistry.plugins)
def get_processor(plugin_type: str, config: dict) -> BasePlugin:
    """
    Retrieves a plugin instance by its type.
    """
```

```
plugin_class = PluginRegistry.plugins.get(plugin_type)
if not plugin_class:
        raise ValueError(f"No plugin found for type:
{plugin_type}")
return plugin_class(config)

image_processor = get_processor("image", {"width": 100,
"height": 100})
text_processor = get_processor("text", {"encoding": "utf-8"})

image_processor.process("image_data")
text_processor.process("text_data")
```

- In this example, the PluginRegistry metaclass automatically registers any class that uses it (or its subclasses) and has the attribute plugin_type.
  This registration occurs during class creation, eliminating the need for manual registration.
  The get_processor function can then retrieve the appropriate processor.

## 2.2. Decorators for Extension Configuration

- **Decorators** can be used to further customize or configure extension classes.
  - ○ They can add attributes, methods, or modify existing ones.
  - ○ They provide a way to apply specific configurations or enhancements to individual extensions.

- **Example: Configuring Plugins with a Decorator**

```python
from typing import Callable, TypeVar, ParamSpec, Any
import functools

P = ParamSpec('P')
R = TypeVar('R')

def plugin_config(enabled: bool = True, priority: int = 100) ->
Callable[[type[Any]], type[Any]]:
    """
    A decorator to configure plugins.
    """
    def decorator(cls: type[Any]) -> type:
        cls.enabled = enabled  # Add 'enabled' attribute
        cls.priority = priority  # Add 'priority' attribute
        return cls
    return decorator

class PluginRegistry(type):
    plugins: dict[str, type] = {}

    def __new__(cls, name, bases, dct):
        plugin_class = super().__new__(cls, name, bases, dct)
        if hasattr(plugin_class, "get_plugin_type"):
            PluginRegistry.plugins[plugin_class.get_plugin_type()]
= plugin_class
        return plugin_class

class BasePlugin(metaclass=PluginRegistry):
    def __init__(self, config):
```

```python
        self.config = config

    @classmethod
    @abc.abstractmethod
    def get_plugin_type(cls) -> str:
        return cls.plugin_type
@plugin_config(enabled=True, priority=1)
class HighPriorityPlugin(BasePlugin):
    plugin_type = "high_priority"
    def process(self, data):
        return f"HighPriorityPlugin processed: {data}"
@plugin_config(enabled=False, priority=10)
class LowPriorityPlugin(BasePlugin):
    plugin_type = "low_priority"

    def process(self, data):
        return f"LowPriorityPlugin processed: {data}"

enabled_plugins = [
    plugin
    for plugin in PluginRegistry.plugins.values()
    if getattr(plugin, "enabled", True)
]
for plugin_class in sorted(enabled_plugins, key=lambda p: getattr(p, "priority", 100)):

    print(f"Enabled Plugin: {plugin_class.__name__}")
```

In this example, the @plugin_config decorator adds enabled and priority attributes to plugin classes. This allows you to configure which plugins are loaded and in what order they are used.

### 3. Benefits of Combining Metaclasses and Decorators

- **Clear Separation of Concerns**: Metaclasses handle automatic registration and interface enforcement, while decorators handle the configuration of individual plugins.
- **Reduced Boilerplate**: Developers creating new plugins only need to define the plugin's core logic and apply the configuration decorator.
- **Enhanced Flexibility**: Decorators provide a flexible way to customize individual plugins, while metaclasses ensure consistency across all plugins.
- **Adaptable Systems**: Easily add or remove plugins, or change their configuration, without modifying the application's core.

## *HERE ARE MORE EXAMPLES & CODE SNIPPETS TO SOLIDIFY YOUR UNDERSTANDING OF AUTOMATING EXTENSION MECHANISMS WITH METACLASSES AND DECORATORS (EXAMPLES)*

Let's dive into more detailed examples of how metaclasses and decorators can be used to automate extension mechanisms, building upon the concepts introduced earlier.

### 1. Using Metaclasses and Decorators for Plugin Systems

- **Scenario:** You're building a framework where users can extend functionality by creating plugins. You want to:
  - ○ Automatically register plugins when they are defined.
  - ○ Allow plugin developers to easily configure their plugins.
  - ○ Ensure that all plugins adhere to a common interface.
- **Solution:** Combine a metaclass for registration with a decorator for configuration.
- **Example:**

```python
import abc
from typing import Callable, TypeVar, ParamSpec, Any, Dict

P = ParamSpec('P')
R = TypeVar('R')

class PluginRegistry(type):
    """
    A metaclass that automatically registers plugins.
    """

    plugins: Dict[str, type] = {}  # Class-level registry of plugins

    def __new__(cls, name, bases, dct):
        plugin_class = super().__new__(cls, name, bases, dct) # Create the class
        if hasattr(plugin_class, "get_plugin_type"):
            PluginRegistry.plugins[plugin_class.get_plugin_type()] = plugin_class # Register by plugin_type
```

```python
        return plugin_class

def plugin_config(
    enabled: bool = True,
    priority: int = 100,
) -> Callable[[type[Any]], type[Any]]:
    """
    A decorator to configure plugins.
    """

    def decorator(cls: type[Any]) -> type:
        """Adds configuration attributes to the class."""
        cls.enabled = enabled  # Add 'enabled' attribute
        cls.priority = priority  # Add 'priority' attribute
        return cls

    return decorator

class BasePlugin(metaclass=PluginRegistry):
    """
    Base class for all plugins.
    """

    def __init__(self, config: Dict[str, Any]):
        """Initializes the plugin with configuration."""
        self.config = config

    @classmethod
    @abc.abstractmethod
    def get_plugin_type(cls) -> str:
```

```python
        """Returns the type of plugin."""
        return cls.plugin_type

    @abc.abstractmethod
    def process(self, data: Any) -> Any:
        """Processes the input data."""
        raise NotImplementedError("Subclasses must implement
the process method")

@plugin_config(enabled=True, priority=1)
class ImageProcessor(BasePlugin):
    """
    A plugin for processing images.
    """

    plugin_type = "image"  # Plugin type for registration

    def __init__(self, config: Dict[str, Any]):
        super().__init__(config)
        self.width = self.config.get("width", 200)
        self.height = self.config.get("height", 200)

    def process(self, data: bytes) -> bytes:
        """Processes image data."""
        print(
                f"Processing image with width={self.width},
height={self.height} and config: {self.config}"
        )
        return b"Processed image data: " + data
```

```python
@plugin_config(enabled=False, priority=10)
class TextProcessor(BasePlugin):
    """

    A plugin for processing text.
    """

    plugin_type = "text"  # Plugin type for registration

    def __init__(self, config: Dict[str, Any]):
        super().__init__(config)
        self.encoding = self.config.get("encoding", "utf-8")

    def process(self, text: str) -> str:
        """Processes text data."""
        return f"Processed text with encoding {self.encoding}: {text}"

# Load and use plugins
enabled_plugins = [
    plugin_class
    for plugin_class in PluginRegistry.plugins.values()
    if getattr(plugin_class, "enabled", True)
]

# Sort plugins by priority (lower number means higher priority)
sorted_plugins = sorted(enabled_plugins, key=lambda p: getattr(p, "priority", 100))

for plugin_class in sorted_plugins:
```

```
   plugin_instance = plugin_class({"app_name": "my_app"})
# Create an instance of the plugin
  if plugin_class.get_plugin_type() == "image":
    image_data = b"image_data"
    result = plugin_instance.process(image_data)
    print(result)
  elif plugin_class.get_plugin_type() == "text":
    text_data = "text_data_to_process"
    result = plugin_instance.process(text_data)
    print(result)
```

## *Creating    Configuration-Driven    Applications    with Metaprogramming*

A configuration-driven application is one whose behavior and structure are determined by external configuration data rather than hardcoded logic. Metaprogramming, with its ability to manipulate code at runtime, provides powerful techniques for building such applications, enhancing their adaptability and flexibility.

### 1. The Traditional Approach vs. Metaprogramming

- **Traditional Approach:**
  - Application behavior is defined directly in the code.
  - Changes in behavior often require modifying the code and redeploying the application.
- **Configuration-Driven with Metaprogramming:**

○ Application behavior is defined in external configuration files (e.g., JSON, YAML, Python scripts).
○ The application uses metaprogramming to read the configuration and adapt its behavior accordingly at runtime.

## 2. Benefits of Configuration-Driven Applications with Metaprogramming

- **Adaptability:** The application can adapt to different environments, user needs, or changing requirements without code modifications.
- **Extensibility:** New features or modules can be added by simply updating the configuration.
- **Flexibility:** The application can be customized without recompilation or redeployment.
- **Maintainability:** Configuration is separated from code, making it easier to manage and update.

## 3. Techniques

Here are some metaprogramming techniques you can use to create configuration-driven applications:

- **Dynamic Class and Object Creation:**
  ○ Use type() to create classes dynamically based on configuration data.
  ○ This allows you to define the structure of your application's objects at runtime.

- Dynamic Code Execution with exec() or eval():
  - Execute code snippets or expressions from the configuration to define application logic.
  - This provides maximum flexibility but requires careful attention to security.
- **Metaclasses:**
  - Customize the class creation process to enforce configuration requirements or automatically add functionality based on configuration.
- **Descriptors:**
  - Define managed attributes that retrieve their values from the configuration, enabling lazy loading or dynamic updates.

## 4. Examples

- **Example 1: Dynamic Class Creation from JSON Configuration**

```python
import json

def create_object_from_config(config_file):
    """
    Creates an object dynamically based on a JSON configuration file.
    """
    with open(config_file, "r") as f:
        config_data = json.load(f)

        class_name = config_data.get("class_name", "DynamicObject")
```

```python
    attributes = config_data.get("attributes", {})

    # Dynamically create a class
    DynamicClass = type(class_name, (object,), {})

    def __init__(self, *args, **kwargs):
        """Dynamically generated __init__ method."""
        for i, (attr_name, attr_type) in enumerate(attributes.items()):
            if i < len(args):
                setattr(self, attr_name, args[i])
            elif attr_name in kwargs:
                setattr(self, attr_name, kwargs[attr_name])
            else:
                setattr(self, attr_name, None)

    DynamicClass.__init__ = __init__

    # Add attributes to the class
    for attr_name, attr_type in attributes.items():
        setattr(DynamicClass, attr_name, None)

    instance = DynamicClass()
    return instance

# config.json:
# {
#     "class_name": "MyConfiguredClass",
#     "attributes": {
#         "param1": "str",
```

```
#       "param2": "int",
#       "param3": "list"
#   }
# }

my_object = create_object_from_config("config.json")
my_object.param1 = "hello"
my_object.param2 = 123
my_object.param3 = [1, 2, 3]

print(my_object.param1,                      my_object.param2,
my_object.param3)
```

- This example reads a JSON file to get the class name and attributes, then uses type() to create the class dynamically.
- Example 2: Using eval() for Dynamic Logic

```
def process_data(data, config):
    """Processes data based on a dynamically evaluated
expression from config."""
    processing_logic = config.get("processing_logic", "data") #
Default to 'data'
    try:
        result = eval(processing_logic, {}, {"data": data}) #
Evaluate in a safe context
        return result
    except Exception as e:
        raise ValueError(f"Invalid processing logic:
{processing_logic}") from e
```

```
# Configuration is passed as a dictionary
config1 = {"processing_logic": "data.upper()"}
config2 = {"processing_logic": "len(data)"}
config3 = {"processing_logic": "data[1:3]"}

data_to_process = "hello"
processed_data1 = process_data(data_to_process, config1)  #
result is HELLO
processed_data2 = process_data(data_to_process, config2)  #
result is 5
processed_data3 = process_data(data_to_process, config3)  #
result is el

print(processed_data1)
print(processed_data2)
print(processed_data3)
```

- In this example, the process_data function uses an expression from the configuration to determine how to process the input data. The expression is evaluated using eval(), allowing for dynamic behavior.

## 5. Best Practices

- **Externalize Configuration:** Store configuration data in formats like JSON, YAML, or dedicated configuration files.
- **Use Safe Evaluation:** If you must use eval(), do so with extreme caution. Restrict the namespaces to only the necessary variables and functions.

- **Validate Configuration:** Validate the configuration data to ensure it conforms to the expected structure and values.
- **Design for Flexibility:** Structure your application to make it easy to add new configuration options or extend existing ones.
- **Document Configuration Options:** Clearly document the available configuration options and their effects on the application's behavior.

## *Case Studies of Extensible Python Applications*

Metaprogramming techniques, such as decorators and metaclasses, enable developers to design applications that are inherently extensible. Here are some case studies of Python applications that exemplify this approach:

### 1. Django's ORM (Object-Relational Mapper)

- **Extensibility Challenge:** Django, a popular web framework, needs to support a wide variety of database systems (e.g., PostgreSQL, MySQL, SQLite) and allow developers to define custom data models.
- **Metaprogramming Solution:** Django's ORM uses metaclasses to dynamically generate the mapping between Python classes and database tables.
  - When you define a Django model:

```python
from django.db import models

class MyModel(models.Model):

    name = models.CharField(max_length=100)
```

```
age = models.IntegerField()
```

- o Django's metaclasses inspect the fields you define (e.g., CharField, IntegerField) and use this information to:
  - Create the corresponding database table schema.
  - Generate methods for querying and manipulating data.
- **Extensibility Benefits:**
  - o **Database Abstraction:** Django can work with different databases without requiring changes to your model definitions.
  - o **Dynamic Model Creation:** You can define your models in a Pythonic way, and Django handles the database interactions.
  - o **Custom Field Types:** Developers can create custom field types, which Django's ORM can then incorporate into the database schema.
- **References:**
  - o Django ORM Documentation

## 2. Flask Web Framework

- **Extensibility Challenge:** Flask, a micro web framework, needs to be lightweight and flexible, allowing developers to add functionality as needed.
- **Metaprogramming Solution:** Flask uses decorators extensively to map URLs to view functions and add functionality to routes.
  - o Example:

```python
from flask import Flask

app = Flask(__name__)

@app.route("/")  # Decorator for URL routing
def hello():
    return "Hello, World!"

@app.route("/user/<username>")  # Route with a parameter
def show_user_profile(username):
    return f"User: {username}"
```

- Flask uses decorators like @app.route() to extend the functionality of view functions, making it easy to add new routes and customize request handling.
- **Extensibility Benefits:**
  - **Modular Design:** Flask remains lightweight, and developers can add extensions for specific features (e.g., authentication, database integration).
  - **Flexible Routing:** URL routing is handled dynamically through decorators.
  - **Easy Extension:** Developers can create their own decorators to add custom functionality to view functions.
- **References:**
  - Flask Documentation on Routing

## 3. Pytest Plugin System

- **Extensibility Challenge:** Pytest, a testing framework, needs to support a wide range of testing needs and allow users to customize its behavior.
- **Metaprogramming Solution:** Pytest uses a plugin system that relies on dynamic discovery and loading of plugins.
    - Pytest discovers plugins by:
        - Importing modules that match certain naming conventions.
        - Looking for functions with specific names (e.g., pytest_configure, pytest_addoption) that act as hooks.
    - Users can create custom plugins by:
        - Defining new hook functions.
        - Implementing the pytest plugin interface.
- **Extensibility Benefits:**
    - **Highly Customizable:** Users can extend pytest to support custom testing frameworks, reporting mechanisms, and test collection strategies.
    - **Large Plugin Ecosystem:** A wide variety of third-party plugins are available, providing functionality for specific testing needs.
    - **Dynamic Behavior:** Pytest adapts its behavior based on the installed and activated plugins.
- **References:**
    - Pytest Plugin System

*LET'S EXPLORE SOME MORE DETAILED EXAMPLES OF HOW PYTHON APPLICATIONS LEVERAGE METAPROGRAMMING FOR EXTENSIBILITY:*

# 1. Celery Task Queue

- **Extensibility Challenge:** Celery is a distributed task queue used to execute asynchronous tasks. It needs to support various message brokers (e.g., RabbitMQ, Redis) and allow users to define custom task execution logic.
- **Metaprogramming Solution:**
  - **Dynamic Task Definition:** Celery allows users to define tasks as regular Python functions, which Celery then wraps and manages. This is achieved through decorators and function introspection.
  - **Custom Components:** Celery allows you to create custom components like task schedulers, consumers, and result stores.
- **Example:**

```python
from celery import Celery
from celery import Task
import time

# Initialize Celery
app = Celery('my_app', broker='redis://localhost:6379')

#Register a task
@app.task
def add(x, y):
    """An asynchronous task that adds two numbers."""
    print(f"Adding {x} + {y}")
    time.sleep(2)  # Simulate some work
    return x + y
```

```
#register a class based task
class MyTask(Task):
  def run(self, x, y):
    print(f"running MyTask: x:{x}, y:{y}")
    return x + y
app.register_task(MyTask)

# Call the task asynchronously
result = add.delay(2, 3)
print(f"Task sent. Result will be available later: {result}")
```

- In this example, the @app.task decorator transforms the add function into an asynchronous task. Celery's worker processes then execute this task.
- **Extensibility Benefits:**
    - ○ **Broker and Backend Flexibility:** Celery can work with different message brokers and result backends through a plugin system.
    - ○ **Customizable Workers:** Celery workers can be extended to support custom task execution logic.
    - ○ **Task Routing:** Celery provides flexible mechanisms for routing tasks to different queues and workers.

## 2. SQLAlchemy

- **Extensibility Challenge:** SQLAlchemy is a powerful SQL toolkit and ORM. It needs to support a wide variety of database systems and allow users to define complex data mappings and relationships.

- **Metaprogramming Solution:**
  - **Dynamic Type System:** SQLAlchemy's type system allows you to define custom data types that map to specific database types.
  - **Custom Dialects:** SQLAlchemy supports different database systems through dialects, which can be extended or customized.
  - **Metaclasses and Declarative System:** SQLAlchemy's ORM uses a declarative system, which employs metaclasses to automatically generate table mappings and relationships based on user-defined classes.
- **Example:**

```
from sqlalchemy import create_engine, Column, Integer, String
from sqlalchemy.ext.declarative import declarative_base
from sqlalchemy.orm import sessionmaker

# Define the database engine
engine = create_engine('sqlite:///:memory:')   # In-memory SQLite database

# Declare a base class for declarative models
Base = declarative_base()

class User(Base):
    __tablename__ = 'users'
    id = Column(Integer, primary_key=True)
    name = Column(String)
    age = Column(Integer)
```

```python
    def __repr__(self):
        return f"User(name={self.name}, age={self.age})"

# Create the table in the database
Base.metadata.create_all(engine)

# Create a session to interact with the database
Session = sessionmaker(bind=engine)
session = Session()

# Create and add a user
new_user = User(name='Alice', age=30)
session.add(new_user)
session.commit()

# Query the database
users = session.query(User).all()
for user in users:
    print(user)
```

- **Extensibility Benefits:**
  - **Database Abstraction:** SQLAlchemy provides a consistent interface for working with different databases.
  - **Type Extensibility:** Developers can define custom data types.
  - **ORM Flexibility:** The declarative system and metaclasses make it easy to define complex database mappings.
- **References:**

- SQLAlchemy Documentation

# CHAPTER 9

## *Advanced Metaprogramming Techniques and Best Practices*

*Runtime Code Generation and Modification in Python*

Runtime code generation and modification involve creating or altering code while a program is running. This advanced technique allows for highly dynamic and adaptable applications but also introduces significant complexity and potential risks. Here's a breakdown of the core concepts and techniques:

### 1. Runtime Code Generation

- **Definition:** The process of constructing new code (e.g., functions, classes, modules) during the execution of a program. The generated code didn't exist in the program's source code when it was initially written.
- **Techniques:**
    - exec() and eval(): As discussed in previous sections, these built-in functions can execute code from strings. You can construct strings containing

Python code and then use these functions to run them.

- ○ The type() function: As we saw when discussing metaclasses, the type function can be used to create new classes dynamically. This is a form of code generation, as you're constructing a new class object at runtime.
- ○ **Abstract Syntax Trees (ASTs):** The ast module allows you to create and manipulate ASTs, which represent the structure of Python code. You can programmatically construct an AST and then compile it into a code object that can be executed.
- **Libraries:**
  - ○ Jinja2: A powerful templating engine often used for generating HTML, but it can also generate Python code. You define templates with placeholders, and then render them with specific data to produce Python code strings.
  - ○ codegen: A small Python library to generate Python source code.

## 2. Runtime Code Modification

- **Definition:** The process of altering the structure or behavior of existing code while the program is running.
- **Techniques:**
  - ○ **Descriptors:** As discussed earlier, descriptors provide a way to manage attribute access. You can use them to dynamically alter how attributes are

accessed or set, effectively modifying the behavior of objects.

- o **Metaclasses:** By customizing metaclasses, you can control the class creation process and modify class behavior, attributes, or methods. Since classes define the behavior of their instances, this is a powerful form of code modification.
- o setattr(): The setattr() built-in function allows you to set the attribute of an object. This can be used to add new attributes or modify existing ones of a class instance.

## 3. Bytecode Manipulation

- **Definition:** Python code is compiled into bytecode before being executed by the Python Virtual Machine (PVM). Bytecode manipulation involves directly modifying this bytecode.
- **Libraries:**
  - o dis: The dis module allows you to disassemble Python code into bytecode instructions, making it somewhat readable.
  - o opcode: The opcode module provides functions to work with Python bytecodes.
- **Complexity and Risk:** Bytecode manipulation is a very low-level and complex technique. It's easy to corrupt the code and cause unpredictable behavior or crashes. It also makes your code less portable, as bytecode can vary between Python versions. It should be used only in very

rare and specific cases where other higher-level techniques are insufficient.

## 4. Use Cases

- **Dynamic Proxies:** Create proxy objects that intercept and modify interactions with other objects.
- **Dynamic APIs:** Generate API endpoints or client libraries based on metadata or specifications.
- **Hot Reloading:** Reload code in a running application without restarting it.
- **Custom Language Features:** Implement custom language features or DSLs.
- **AOP (Aspect-Oriented Programming):** While Python doesn't have native AOP, you can use metaprogramming to achieve similar results.

## 5. Example: Dynamic Function Modification with Bytecode Manipulation (Advanced)

- **Disclaimer:** This is a very advanced and potentially dangerous technique. Handle with extreme care and ensure you thoroughly understand the implications.

```python
import types
import dis
import opcode
import sys


def modify_function_bytecode(func, new_code):
    """

    Modifies the bytecode of a function.
```

```
    Args:
        func: The function to modify.
            new_code: A compiled code object with the new
bytecode.
    """

    if not isinstance(func, types.FunctionType):
        raise TypeError("Expected a function")

    func.__code__ = new_code

def add_print_before(original_function):
    """
    Prepends a print statement to a function's bytecode
    """

        original_code = original_function.__code__

    #get the constants
    consts = list(original_code.co_consts)

    #insert the string
    consts.insert(0, f"Calling {original_function.__name__}")

    #construct new code string
    new_code_bytes = b"
                                new_code_bytes      +=
bytes([opcode.opmap['LOAD_GLOBAL'], 0, 0])    # Load
global 'print'
```

```python
    new_code_bytes += bytes([opcode.opmap['LOAD_CONST'], 0, 0])  # Load the string
    new_code_bytes += bytes([opcode.opmap['CALL_FUNCTION'], 0x01, 0]) # Call print with one argument

    new_code_bytes += original_code.co_code

    new_code = original_code.replace(co_code=new_code_bytes, co_consts = tuple(consts))

    modify_function_bytecode(original_function, new_code)
    return original_function

def example_function(x, y):
    return x + y
add_print_before(example_function)            #      Modify example_function

example_function(1, 2)
```

## Considerations for Performance and Debugging in Metaprogramming

Metaprogramming, while powerful, can introduce performance overhead and debugging challenges if not used carefully. Here's a breakdown of the key considerations:

## 1. Performance Considerations

- **Increased Complexity:** Metaprogramming often involves writing code that is more abstract and complex than standard procedural or object-oriented code. This added complexity can sometimes lead to performance overhead.
- **Runtime Overhead:** Techniques like dynamic code generation (e.g., using exec() or eval()) and AST manipulation incur a runtime cost. The interpreter needs to parse, compile, and execute code that is generated on the fly, which can be slower than executing pre-compiled code.
- **Metaclass Impact:** Custom metaclasses can affect the class creation process, potentially adding overhead, especially if complex logic is involved. However, the impact is usually felt only during class definition, not during instance creation.
- **Descriptor Overhead:** While descriptors offer powerful attribute management, they can introduce a small performance overhead compared to simple attribute access, as the __get__, __set__, and __delete__ methods need to be called. However, this overhead is often negligible compared to the benefits they provide in terms of code clarity and maintainability.
- **Mitigation Strategies:**
  - **Profile Your Code:** If you suspect that metaprogramming is causing performance bottlenecks, use Python's profiling tools (e.g., cProfile) to identify the specific areas that are consuming the most time.

- Optimize Code Generation: If you're generating code dynamically, try to optimize the code generation process. For example, if you're generating a large amount of code, consider using more efficient string concatenation techniques or pre-compiling code snippets.
- Cache Results: If your metaprogramming involves computations, consider caching the results to avoid redundant calculations.
- Use Metaclasses Judiciously: Use metaclasses only when necessary. Overusing them can lead to unnecessary complexity and potential performance overhead.
- Be Mindful of Complexity: Strive to keep your metaprogramming code as clear and simple as possible to minimize its performance impact.

## 2. Debugging Challenges

Metaprogramming can make debugging more challenging due to its dynamic nature and increased level of abstraction.

- **Dynamic Code:** When code is generated or modified at runtime, it can be harder to trace the execution flow and understand the code that is actually being executed.
- **Abstraction:** Metaprogramming techniques like decorators and metaclasses add layers of abstraction, which can make it more difficult to follow the logic of your code.
- **Tracebacks:** Tracebacks can be less informative in metaprogramming scenarios, especially when dealing

with dynamically generated code or modified class structures.

- **Strategies:**
  - **Print Statements:** Use print statements strategically to inspect the values of variables and the flow of execution within your metaprogramming code.
  - **Logging:** Employ Python's logging module to record detailed information about the execution of your metaprogramming code. This can be invaluable for understanding the sequence of events and identifying the source of errors.
  - **pdb (Python Debugger):** Use the pdb module to step through your code, set breakpoints, and inspect variables. This can help you understand how your metaprogramming code is being executed.
  - Introspection with inspect: Use the inspect module to examine the structure of objects, functions, and classes at runtime. This can help you understand the state of your code and identify unexpected behavior.
  - **AST Dumps:** When working with ASTs, use ast.dump() to print the tree structure and verify that it is being generated and modified as expected.
  - **Isolate and Simplify:** When debugging metaprogramming code, try to isolate the problematic part and simplify it as much as possible to narrow down the source of the issue.

○ **Thorough Testing:** Write comprehensive unit and integration tests to ensure that your metaprogramming code works correctly and doesn't introduce unexpected side effects.

### *Best Practices for Writing Maintainable and Understandable Metaprogramming Code*

Metaprogramming, while powerful, can significantly increase the complexity of your code. Following best practices is crucial to ensure that your metaprogramming code remains maintainable, readable, and less prone to errors.

### 1. Prioritize Clarity and Readability

- **Write Clean Code:** Strive to write metaprogramming code that is as clear and concise as possible. Use meaningful names for variables, functions, and classes.
- **Use Comments Liberally:** Metaprogramming can be tricky to understand, so comments are essential. Explain the purpose of your decorators, metaclasses, or AST manipulations. Document the expected input and output, and provide rationale for your design choices.
- **Follow Naming Conventions:** Adhere to Python's naming conventions (PEP 8) to maintain consistency and readability. Consider adding a suffix like Meta to your metaclass names (e.g., MyClassMeta) to clearly identify them.
- **Keep Functions Short and Focused:** Break down complex metaprogramming logic into smaller, more manageable functions. This improves readability and makes debugging easier.

## 2. Minimize Complexity

- **Avoid Over-Engineering:** Don't use metaprogramming for simple tasks that can be achieved with standard Python constructs. Overusing metaprogramming can make your code harder to understand and maintain.
- **Prefer Simpler Alternatives:** Before resorting to advanced techniques like metaclasses or AST manipulation, consider if simpler alternatives like function decorators or class factories can solve your problem.
- **Use the Least Powerful Tool:** Choose the least powerful tool that meets your needs. For example, if you only need to modify a class's attributes, a class decorator is often simpler and more readable than a metaclass.

## 3. Thorough Documentation

- **Document Decorators:** Clearly explain the purpose of each decorator, what it does to the decorated function or class, and any potential side effects.
- **Document Metaclasses:** Provide detailed documentation for your metaclasses, explaining how they modify class creation and what behavior they enforce.
- **Document AST Transformations:** If you're manipulating ASTs, document the structure of the AST you're working with and the transformations you're applying.
- **Use Docstrings:** Use docstrings to explain the purpose, arguments, and return values of your metaprogramming functions and classes.

## 4. Robust Error Handling

- **Handle Exceptions:** Include appropriate error handling (e.g., try...except blocks) to catch potential exceptions during dynamic code execution or AST manipulation. Provide informative error messages to help with debugging.
- **Validate Inputs:** If your metaprogramming code relies on external input (e.g., configuration data, user input), validate that input to ensure it conforms to the expected format and values. This can prevent unexpected errors or security vulnerabilities.
- **Fail Early:** If you detect an error during the code generation or modification process, raise an exception as soon as possible to prevent further execution with invalid code.

## 5. Testing

- **Write Unit Tests:** Thoroughly test your metaprogramming code with unit tests. This includes testing the behavior of your decorators, metaclasses, and AST transformations.
- **Test Generated Code:** If you're generating code dynamically, write tests to ensure that the generated code is correct and produces the expected results.
- **Test Edge Cases:** Consider testing edge cases and unusual scenarios to ensure that your metaprogramming code is robust and handles unexpected situations gracefully.

## 6. Security Best Practices

- **Avoid Executing Untrusted Code:** If your metaprogramming code involves dynamic code execution (e.g., with exec() or eval()), never execute code from untrusted sources. This is a major security risk.
- **Restrict Namespaces:** When using exec() or eval(), always pass in carefully constructed globals and locals dictionaries to limit the code's access to variables and functions in your program.
- **Sanitize Inputs:** If you're generating code based on user input or external data, sanitize that input to prevent code injection attacks.
- **Use Secure Alternatives:** If possible, use safer alternatives to dynamic code execution, such as template engines or DSLs with restricted syntax.

By following these best practices, you can write metaprogramming code that is not only powerful but also maintainable, understandable, and secure.

## *Potential Pitfalls and Anti-Patterns to Avoid in Metaprogramming*

Metaprogramming, while a powerful tool, can also introduce complexity and potential problems if not used carefully. Here are some common pitfalls and anti-patterns to avoid:

### 1. Overuse of Metaprogramming

- Pitfall: Using metaprogramming for tasks that can be solved more simply with standard Python constructs.

- Consequences:
  - Increased Complexity: Metaprogramming often involves more intricate code than traditional programming, making it harder to understand and maintain.
  - Reduced Readability: Code that uses metaprogramming can be less intuitive and more difficult for other developers to follow.
  - Debugging Challenges: Debugging metaprogramming code can be more challenging due to its dynamic nature.
- Best Practice:
  - Keep it Simple: Use metaprogramming only when it provides a significant advantage in terms of flexibility, extensibility, or code reuse.
  - Prefer Simpler Alternatives: If a problem can be solved with simpler language features (e.g., functions, class inheritance, composition), use those instead.

## 2. Excessive Dynamic Code Generation

- Pitfall: Generating large amounts of code dynamically, especially based on complex logic or external input.
- Consequences:
  - Performance Overhead: Dynamic code generation involves runtime parsing and compilation, which can be expensive.

- Readability Issues: Dynamically generated code can be hard to read and understand, especially if it's not well-structured.
- Debugging Difficulties: It can be challenging to debug code that is generated on the fly, as it may not be present in the source code.
- Best Practice:
  - Minimize Dynamic Code Generation: Generate only the necessary parts of the code dynamically.
  - Use Templates: For generating code with a consistent structure, consider using templating engines (e.g., Jinja2) to improve readability.
  - Compile Code Objects: If you need to execute the same code multiple times, compile it into a code object using the compile() function for better performance.
  - Consider Alternatives: Explore alternatives such as using data structures or configuration files.

## 3. Ignoring Security Risks

- Pitfall: Executing untrusted code with exec() or eval().
- Consequences:
  - Code Injection Attacks: Attackers can inject malicious code into the input string, potentially leading to severe security vulnerabilities.
  - System Compromise: Malicious code can execute arbitrary commands, access sensitive data, or even take control of the system.
- Best Practice:

- Never execute untrusted code: If the code you're passing to exec() or eval() comes from an external source (e.g., user input, network requests), it is considered untrusted.
- Restrict namespaces: If you must use exec() or eval(), always pass in carefully constructed globals and locals dictionaries to limit the code's access to variables and functions.
- Sanitize inputs: If you're generating code based on user-provided data, sanitize the input to remove any potentially dangerous code constructs.
- Use safer alternatives: Explore safer ways to achieve the desired functionality, such as using a restricted DSL or a dedicated parser.

## 4. Overly Complex Metaclasses

- Pitfall: Creating metaclasses with excessive logic or intricate manipulations of class attributes.
- Consequences:
  - Reduced Readability: Complex metaclasses can be very difficult to understand, even for experienced developers.
  - Increased Maintenance Burden: They can be challenging to modify or debug, making the codebase harder to maintain.
  - Unexpected Behavior: Subtle errors in metaclass logic can lead to unexpected and hard-to-diagnose behavior in the classes they create.
- Best Practice:

- Keep Metaclasses Simple: Metaclasses should ideally handle only essential class creation logic.
- Delegate Complexity: If you need to add significant functionality to classes, consider using class decorators or other techniques in conjunction with metaclasses.
- Document Thoroughly: If you must use complex metaclasses, provide comprehensive documentation explaining their behavior and purpose.

## 5. Lack of Clear Abstraction

- Pitfall: Mixing metaprogramming logic with the core logic of your application, leading to tangled and difficult-to-understand code.
- Consequences:
  - Reduced Modularity: Code becomes less organized and harder to reason about.
  - Increased Coupling: Different parts of the application become tightly coupled, making it harder to modify them independently.
  - Maintenance Difficulties: Changes in one part of the code can have unintended consequences in other parts.
- Best Practice:
  - Separate Concerns: Keep your metaprogramming code separate from your application's core logic.
  - Define Clear Interfaces: Use abstract base classes or protocols to define clear interfaces for any code

that interacts with your metaprogramming constructs.
- o Use Modular Design: Structure your application into modules or packages that encapsulate specific functionalities, including any metaprogramming code.

By adhering to these anti-patterns and following the best practices, you can leverage the power of metaprogramming while minimizing its drawbacks, resulting in more robust, maintainable, and understandable Python code.

www.ingramcontent.com/pod-product-compliance
Lightning Source LLC
Chambersburg PA
CBHW080550060326
40689CB00021B/4805